Advance Praise
for
Have Fun. Learn Stuff. Grow.
Homeschooling and the Curriculum of Love

"One of the most dynamic and prolific homeschooling writers today is David Albert, homeschooling father of two, popular speaker at conferences across the nation, regular columnist for two major homeschooling publications, and author of two of the most highly acclaimed homeschooling books ever published—*And the Skylark Sings With Me* and *Homeschooling and the Voyage of Self-Discovery*. Now David has written a book he titles, in a very no-nonsense manner, *Have Fun. Learn Stuff. Grow. Homeschooling and the Curriculum of Love*.

"The title says it all. Almost. David doesn't just write about homeschooling your children. He pokes and prods and questions and insists that you join him in analyzing the whys and wherefores of what you and your kids are doing every day. He wraps his writing in a warm sense of humor and adds plenty of his own life experiences, and somewhere in the middle of reading one of his books you start wondering why it feels as though you are reading the writings of an old friend. It's a comfortable feeling; encouraging, reassuring. Words have power, and David Albert knows how to harness that power and use it to help you help your children become who they are meant to be.

"Have Fun. Learn Stuff. Grow." You'll do all three with David's newest book on homeschooling.

—Helen Hegener, Editor and Publisher,
Home Education Magazine

"As if channeled from the highest archangel, David Albert's new book *Have Fun. Learn Stuff. Grow* offers a fresh, crystal-clear look at the very essence of love and learning, and the critical importance of love for nurturing learning. Insightful, unique, and perceptive, the book is a gift for all homeschooling families and those considering it for the first time."

—Jan Hunt, Author, *The Natural Child: Parenting from the Heart*,
and Director, The Natural Children Project

"My heart leaps up with anticipation when I read David Albert's writing. The wealth of his experience embroiders and highlights the essentially simple, pure-hearted truth he expresses: the value of respect and honor for the minds of young people, fresh beings grappling with this very complicated and often difficult world. David is a skilled wordsmith and a graceful and generous storyteller. Most important to me is his compassionate vision of the possibilities for learning and for relationships that are available to beings of all ages on this planet, and his romping enthusiasm and exuberance about the joys of learning, for all of us, everywhere. David Albert's Curriculum of Love works, and we all know it in the center of our being."

—Joyce Reed, retired Associate Dean, Brown University,
and mother of five homeschooled college graduates

"And I thought it was just another homeschooling book! Not here. *Have Fun. Learn Stuff. Grow.* is a delightful mix of philosophy, metaphor and storytelling, and "how to" homeschool in freedom. But it's not just about or for the kids. Albert challenges you to think about your outlook toward living and then gently, sometimes playfully, often deeply, exposes ways to grow through stories from his own life.

"For readers specifically looking for information about sane attitudes and approaches to math and spelling (and maybe all other "school" subjects), there is entertaining reading that should be mandatory for all parents and teachers. Read this book if you've ever wondered about the power of video games or listened to parents debate their value.

"Have Fun. Learn Stuff. Grow. will force you to stretch your thinking, and expand the context within which you consider your own family's learning endeavors."

—Jean Reed, Author, *The Home School Source Book*

HAVE FUN.

LEARN STUFF.

GROW.

Homeschooling
and the
Curriculum of Love

David H. Albert

Common Courage Press   Monroe, Maine

Copyright 2006 © by David H. Albert

Cover art by Brianna K. Thomas
Cover design by Erica Bjerning

Library of Congress Cataloging-in-Publication Data is available from publisher on request.
ISBN 1-56751-370-0 paper
ISBN 1-56751-371-9 hardcover

Common Courage Press
121 Red Barn Road
Monroe, ME 04951

207-525-0900
fax: 207-525-3068

www.commoncouragepress.com
info@commoncouragepress.com

First Printing
Printed in Canada

E voi, piuttosto che le nostre povere
Gabbane d'istrioni, le nostr'anime
Considerae, poiché siam unomini
Di carne e d'ossa, e che di quest'orfano
Mondo al pari di voi spiriamo l'aere!

Il concerto vi dissi. Or ascoltate
Com'egli è svolto.

Mark well, therefore, our souls,
rather than the poor players' garb
we wear, for we are men of flesh and bone,
like you, breathing the same air of this
orphan world.

This, then, is our design. Now give heed
to its unfolding

—from the Prologue, *I Pagliacci*
by Ruggiero Leoncavallo

Contents

Foreword

Jyotibhai Desai

When I received David's letter (in January 2005) inviting me to write a foreword to his latest book, I had some hesitation on account of my English, which is not my mother tongue. Were I to write in Gujarati, I would have been more at ease, and would perhaps have done this job greater justice.

I have known David, his wife Ellen, and his two children Aliyah and Meera, for a long time, having first met David in 1977. I have had not only the opportunity to read his books, letters, and musings, but also the privilege of having the whole family here with us in Vedcchi, a tribal village in the remote and jungly areas of Surat District in Gujarat in western India. We have a wonderful photo of three-year-old Aliyah with a fully-grown peacock in front of a village home, and so many memories they have shared with us.

Where to begin? At the beginning, I guess. But which one? I am like the first man in the first tale in this book, the one who drifted in a boat upon the ocean to test his theory about ocean currents and early seagoing expeditions.

No seagoing for me, though. I am just a village teacher, with a claim to having long experimented with Mohandas Gandhi's ideas on education, and to having learned to live honestly, for the love of children.

This "plan" probably began with my mother, whose dedication to live an honest and courageous life I have yet to match. When the Salt March—that miracle in history that exposed the injustice of British rule—was initiated by Gandhi, my mother said to my father, "These are not times to live just for the family. Go and join the salt protest. I will look after the children." The youngest was my sister, just a year old, and we three brothers of 9, 7, and 5, I being the youngest. It was a call she felt for all who cared to have their children live in a future free India. The freedom to choose our way in our lives was always there, and we knew that even if there were disagreements, our parents' love and encouragement would always be forthcoming.

I left Bombay, the city of my birth, and where I had been until the age of 24, and went to a village ashram in the district of Ahmedabad. The children of the fifth grade class of the village school claimed me as their teacher, as they did not have one. I was really overjoyed that they wanted me! On the very first day, I declared in the morning assembly, "I believe that to punish a child is not the way to help her learn and, therefore, I hereby want you all to know that I will never ever think of punishing any of you, whatever you do."

The head of the school was very upset. "These are wild children," he said, "and none of your city ways are going to work here. You are a fool to make such a statement here in front of them and us. You will end up creating nothing but trouble."

One of the boys in the class got the message, and devised a challenge to my thinking. In less than a week he managed a way for me to fall in such a manner so that I fractured my right hand. I had to leave for Ahmedabad some 52 miles away, and ended up with my arm in a sling.

On my journey home, I got down from the train at a station several ahead of my destination in order to go to Bhagwat's home, where he had run away after the prank. "Come now. We will go back together and be real friends!" I said. His father had heard what had happened and was surprised I had come to take his son back with me.

Ten years later I was traveling along that same train route and Bhagwat's father saw me. "Oh Jyotibhai, how could you go without visiting us?" I had to change my plans to be with the family for a day. The father was all enthusiastic, all day long talking about his only son Bhagwat. He oft repeated, "*Your* son has achieved much. I thought he would never learn anything, and would waste his life. Hence I sent him to the ashram school. But now he is a responsible police officer." Yes, Bhagwat was my son.

Another ten years passed, and I was in a meeting of the heads of education colleges in the state. One of the heads of a well-reputed college of education asked, "Have you heard of the killing of the police officer Dodiya here in Ahmedabad?"

"Who is this Dodiya?" I wondered and asked.

"Oh, Jyotibhai, your Bhagwat Dodiya was a most responsible and upright police officer. He was responsible for curbing crime and was a terror to bootleggers. Our entire area has become safe since he came here two years ago. He often talked about you and claimed that you were his guru. He was killed by the bootleggers at the insistence of the politicians who joined hands to remove him."

I rushed out to his father and the family. "Welcome, Jyotibhai," exclaimed his father with tears rolling down his face, "I am a happy man! Your son has made our entire clan proud. He gave his life to prove himself. Our village is talking about nothing but his uprightness, and how he made the police force proud. Now peaceful can I leave this world, with everyone talking about his goodness and nobility. I have nothing to offer you, who made him such a brave and honest man."

I have so many stories about my days training teachers for village India, and I would love to share them with you, and the rich rewards that I have received from working with children and with future teachers throughout my life. But you might think it odd that I am writing a foreword to a homeschooling book. Let me assure you it is not. For in contrast with most teacher training institutions, our emphasis has always been on self-learning and group learning, activities and practical work. There is no specificity of the place to learn. The trainees work in an institution that is neither spacebound nor timebound, nor bound to a rigid curriculum. Flexibility and freedom, self-study and group work, observation and activity are the salient features of the training methodology that actively promotes the integration of theory and practice. This has always been the way we have trained teachers, and this is what David offers to you as parents for your children, with the goal of producing lifelong learners, who will enjoy their learning as they go on their way. And our goal has always been to enrich our nation, not only by seeking justice or economic or political benefits for the rural people with whom we work, but to help us attain greatness by challenging the frontiers.

And the beginning is where, as David writes in "Homeschooling and the Curriculum of Love," it must begin. "It has to start with an honoring of a child's uniqueness, the assistance we can be in helping her uncover and cultivate it, and, ultimately, making sure she knows to share it around." It is, as I have come to define education, the help that the present gives to the future. That's really what it is all about.

I have seen even at this distance how David and his family have lived and grown together. In "Distinguished Visitors" (in his previous book *Homeschooling and the Voyage of Self-Discovery*), he writes of the expectation of having children coming to visit, and how he could imagine enriching their sojourn. Now at the end of this volume, he writes of Aliyah leaving home, and his hopes and dreams for her. Currently, we are eagerly awaiting her visit to us this July, when she takes a break from her work doing tsunami rehabilitation in south India (you can read about her work at shantinik.blogspot.com). She is achieving her name Aliyah Shanti—"Peace Arising"—and we are privileged through David's writing to witness her unfolding.

And her sister Meera, too. I was there with Ellen in the midst of arranging her adoption back in Bombay in 1990, and now I have watched her grow as well. I translated her story of how, at age 13, she played a benefit piano recital for the Israeli-Palestinian Families of the Bereaved into Gujarati, and the news of both her great-heartedness and her musical skill have spread far and wide. David's writing provides both hope and examples for all those who love children, and are concerned about their gaining their highest potential, not just for themselves, but for the world. David demonstrates that parents who show by their actions that they believe themselves still to be learners in the art of living can hope to see the commitment of their young people to the ideals and the faith they hold. And lifelong learners who seek to restore and revitalize their communities as well.

I am a believer. I believe that when there is honest effort, whether in loving your child or working to make a better world, there is always a benevolent hand that lifts us up. We are like the pigeon in David's "Noah's Boat and the Pigeon of Peace" at the end of this book, and the decision that results:

> And on that day, God made a decision. From that day forth, when He had a message to send, He wasn't going to entrust it to the biggest, or the strongest, or the kingliest, or the best talker, or the one with the biggest mouth. He was going to make sure to entrust His message to just a regular guy. Nobody special. No doves—nothing fancy-shmancy—just pigeons. Just like me and you.

Just like me and you, you and me, just a village teacher in tribal India writing a foreword to a wonderful book!

Jyotibhai Desai
Vedchhi, Gujarat, India
April 27, 2005

For almost four decades, Jyotibhai and Malini Desai have been the driving force behind Gandhi Vidyapith, among the world's most unique institutions in the training of teachers, located in rural Gujarat in western India. They have been leaders in the development of participatory education, where teachers are strongly embedded in the communities in which they work, and are expected to learn from the people of these communities, and help embody each community's unique strengths and aspirations. David Albert can provide you with directions of how to go visit them, but warns you that it is not for the faint of heart, so be sure to take your children along.

Two Boats

Two boats drift upon the ocean.

The boats are similarly equipped. Both boats lack navigational aids and communication equipment. They have the same and ample amounts of food and water. The solitary men in each of the boats have the same level of basic nautical skills, and both are in similarly good health.

Both men spend forty days upon the ocean, facing the same seas—both rough and gentle—and the same sea squalls, hot sun, and chilly nights. Both travel exactly the same distance in the same amount of time, and arrive in the same port on the same day.

The first man undertook his journey to test his theory about ocean currents and early sea-going expeditions. The second man was unexpectedly shipwrecked and had no idea where he was going, or for how long.

For the first man, the voyage, though exhausting, is a triumph. It carries an inner meaning for him, the execution of a long thought-out plan, the confirmation of a theory, a process of proving his mettle. While he will need some time to recover, he can barely wait until he has the opportunity to set forth upon the ocean again.

For the second man, the landing is the end of a forty-day nightmare, the horrific memory of which will never leave him. He will be scarred forever, never fully healed at least in his mind, and, given the choice, he will never set foot on a boat, or even a beach, again.

Two boats, two men, two identical journeys, and two experiences of the journey that could hardly be more different.

Which journey experience more closely resembles your education…

…or your life?

Homeschooling and the Curriculum of Love

As a former book publisher, I duly understand the obligation placed upon an author that, when he chooses the title for a book, he should be expected to explain it. The problem is, as the author of this one, I am very reluctant to do so.

I would like to believe that the very notion of a curriculum of love should be able to stand on its own, without any need of explication. Love—combined with anything regarding children—is its own testament, and doesn't need some high-fallutin' homeschooling author pontificating about it.

Besides, as I sit down to write this title essay, I immediately recognize it to be an oxymoron. Curriculum of love? Should curriculum and love be allowed to occupy the same phrase? Or even the same universe?

If I allow it, the very notion of a curriculum of love can send me into a reverie. Just imagine: there is a committee of the very best lovers (no sex intended) brought together to consider how to imbue every aspect of education systematically with love. There are departments of love, theoretical and applied, inside graduate schools of education all across the country. Maybe every state would have an Assistant Secretary for Love within its office of public instruction. And then....

And then the vision quickly turns dystopian. Fancy word, opposite of utopian. Textbook manufacturers falling all over themselves. Teacher training courses on the right way to teach love. State educational bureaucrats and love experts sitting on committees to set state-mandated learning objectives. Standardized tests for measuring whether the kids have learned their love lessons at the fourth, seventh, and tenth grade levels, and required for high school graduation. Remedial classes and summer sessions for those who have failed. Conferences on the 'crisis in love education', and calls for 'love curriculum reform'. Comparisons among school districts, between states, between nations on the International Standardized Measurement on the Effectiveness of Curriculum of Love Delivery (ISMECLD) would show up in the newspaper, with school superintendents, governors, or even Presidents falling all over themselves to comment. Let's not even begin to consider what might happen in the case of failing schools!

Curriculum and love, I conclude, can indeed occupy the same sentence.

Love and school, for reasons I hope to explore, and despite the best efforts of tens of thousands of loving, caring schoolteachers (my mother having been one), cannot. That's why this has to be a homeschooling book. It is possible to love more than one person—those of us with more than a single child know that quite well. But you can only love one person at a time, in the totality of who she really is, in her fullness of character, and in her idiosyncrasies.

Indeed, if there is to be a curriculum of love, it has to start with honoring each and every child's uniqueness, the sustenance we can provide in helping her uncover and cultivate it, and, ultimately, making sure she knows to share it around.

When I've done this right, that's what our homeschooling experiences have been all about.

* * * * *

More than a few mothers have told me that the first thing they did when their children were born, whether in the hospital or at home, is check to see that all the body parts were there. They counted the fingers and toes. Some have told me they counted more than once, just to be sure. One or two have even told me of dreams they had before the birth of their children being born without an arm, or a leg, or even a head.

Of course, there are times when infants are born when events have not turned out as parents might have planned. Despite our best efforts, careful prenatal environments making use of the best available information, there are infants who come into the world with handicaps and disabilities that cannot be corrected.

When disabled children are born in hospitals, the best hospitals immediately provide counselors to talk with parents about the educational possibilities that will be open to them, and give them hope regarding their children's futures, provided they attend closely to them. Child psychologists have found that this makes a major difference in the bonding that takes place in the family, and ultimately in maximizing the child's, and the family's, potential.

So I came to wonder why we couldn't make that a practice directed at *all* parents, and began to imagine, if placed in such a position, what I would like to say. (Wouldn't it be great to have a book filled with multiple scripts for the occasion?)

One might go something like this:

"Congratulations on the birth of Sarah. I know you are exhausted! And, let me tell, so is she. It is the end of a long journey for both of you, and the beginning of another, one that I hope will bring both of you nothing but joy!

"Sarah is completely healthy, perfect in every way. Yes, as is true for virtually all of us, likely encoded in her somewhere are a set of genetic anomalies, some of which may manifest themselves over what we can all hope will be a long, happy, and fulfilling lifetime. Some of them are of course simply a function of her parent's heritage. But, and you always need to remember this, Sarah is absolutely unique. There is not another person who has ever existed on this planet who has the same biological makeup that she does, or ever will.

"Now there is something else I need to tell you. It is statistically unlikely that Sarah will win the Nobel Peace Prize, invent the final cure for cancer, attend Harvard, compete in the Olympics, conduct the New York Philharmonic, or become President of the United States. All of these are possible, of course, and I don't see anything just now that is likely to prevent them, and I've seen kids go out and do amazing things. But even if you have dreams and aspirations for your child's future, learn to pay attention to her in the here and now, attending to *her* particular gifts and aspirations.

"I remember when I had my first child. I was filled with fantasies and ideas, and anxieties, too. I never outgrew them all, either. I had fears for the future, fears of what I might miss in providing for my daughter, fears that I would be inadequate as a parent. It took me awhile to feel that I really had everything under control, or at least enough control that I could relax, so that we could grow together.

"But, let me also tell you that fantasies, and ideas, and anxieties are a big part of what love is all about. If you lack these, and I'm sure you don't, you would be lacking in those very qualities that make you human, and which you will pass along to Sarah as part of her inheritance, so that she will learn to love as well.

"There are some things you will not understand about your child...and never will. Sarah is her own soul, and with any luck will outlive you, and visit places in space and time that you in this worldly sphere are simply prohibited from going. Indeed, this is one of the great secrets and paradoxes of parenting—you are preparing your child for a future you yourself will never know.

"Now having taken that in, relax. It really isn't as hard as you think. Treat her as if, out of all the possible parents in the world, Sarah chose you! Literally. There are, in fact, philosophers going as far back as Plato who have believed that children choose their parents. You're it. Take it as an honor, and a responsibility, not that you are a parent (lots of folks can make that claim) but that you were specifically chosen to be the parent of Sarah, at this particular and special moment in time. If you learn to listen and to watch and just be present long enough, time will reveal to you why this was meant to be.

"Be assured: Sarah wouldn't have chosen you if you weren't up to the task. Her very uniqueness, the uniqueness that makes her Sarah—call it the *song* of Sarah—is calling to you, and you will know, know deeply, how to respond to it. Yes, you will learn plenty of techniques, tricks of the parenting trade, maybe even a little bit about education, as the two of you travel this path together. You'll find a great library of books out there (I've written some of them myself!) and a walking library of other parents who will freely share their experiences and wisdom with you—sometimes, perhaps, more freely than you'd ever particularly desire. All that is well and good. But, ultimately, all this is really about is paying good attention. Your ability to be the right parent for Sarah is built into you just as securely as being Sarah is built into herself.

"And just one more thing. Don't neglect who you are just because she has arrived. You are born with that same energy and potential as she, and her birth is an invitation to you to maximize it. There is nothing you can do that will be more important to Sarah than your becoming, fully, the person the Great Creator meant you to be.

"What I have to say now will be the most difficult to remember, or even for you to understand, but is perhaps most important of all. Cherish every moment in your lives together. You will find out soon enough that Sarah's life as a child, with you, will not last all that long. It will be gone almost in the twinkling of an eye, and leave behind for both of you a memory of love that will nourish you both for the rest of your earthly sojourns. Grab hold of all of this love that is available to you, and that you are.

"In Yiddish, at the birth of a child, or at any milestone or acknowledgment of an accomplishment or rite of passage, we say "Mazel Tov". The expression contains within those two little words, two very big ideas. For Mazel Tov means "Congratulations" or "Best wishes on your good fortune!" for something that it has already happened, and indeed we wish you that. But it also means, "Good Luck!" as if you are at a commencement, a renewal, or just seeing the boat off at the pier. So Mazel Tov!"[1]

"It's a new beginning"

* * * * *

I was fortunate enough to extricate myself before insensibility set in.

— Rabindranath Tagore,
Nobel Prize-winning poet and playwright,
on quitting school at 13

The author Leo Buscaglia used to take great pains to point out that, to his way of thinking, the opposite of love is not hate, but apathy. Love and hate, he emphasized, are both expressions of attachment to the object of these strong emotions, but in apathy, there is no attachment.

I do not believe that, for humans, apathy is a natural state, and I would find it hard to imagine that anyone who has spent significant time around young children could deem it is. At bottom, apathy (like poorly directed violence) is an expression of powerlessness, a conclusion having been reached that nothing one does really makes a difference. It is a way of coming to terms with an environment that is inflexible, a feeling that one does not truly count, that all has already been determined. Apathy is hopelessness having failed to find another expression.

If love enlarges us, apathy makes us smaller. Apathetic people—including we ourselves when we are apathetic—feel like we have shrunk. Compared with the expansiveness of our innate gifts, skills, longings, desires, and dreams, we have become Lilliputians, for we have learned that to express these very gifts, talents, and aspirations is more likely to bring us pain rather than joy. And that is the thing: apathy is a learned response, actually one that is difficult to learn, as it drives the individual from her

---

1   The *tov* in Mazel Tov simply means "good". The word *mazel* derives from the Hebrew for the Zodiac *mazalot*, and is associated with an infusion of cosmic energy yet to be delivered. The Talmud cites three life issues directly affected by the *mazalot*—life, children, and livelihood. Wishing someone "Mazel Tov" is an expression of hope that the energy of the universe should only be for our, and the world's, good.

natural state. To produce apathy requires repeated episodes of stress, trauma, and encapsulation in an environment that does not respond to us. For apathy is also an expression of a future expectation that *one is simply not going to be listened to*, and, hence, to act, or simply to express oneself in some other manner is just not worth the trouble.

With rare exceptions (and with due respect and gratefulness for those few teachers who truly are doing their best, and who now often feel under siege as a result of No Child Left Behind), schools as we know them are veritable apathy-inducing machines. I use the term "machine" advisedly, for it is the very design of the productive apparatus (rather than the people who operate it, apathetic or otherwise) that forges and then finely hones the final product.

The varieties of *not-listening*[2] begin with the requirement that lesson plans and requirements and expected outcomes be designated before a teacher meets any particular child. No accounting is to be made of what the child knows, or does not know, for indeed, if she knew what was to be taught before the beginning of the school year, what possible sense could be made out of the requirement that the child be enrolled at all?

It is assumed that all children will learn whatever is being taught at the same rate, at the time it is being taught, and that failure will be defined as inability to learn on this timetable. The truth of the matter is that most educators appreciate that children do not learn this way, so the content must be drilled again and again. A system of inflexible pre-determined curricula pretty much assures apathy born of tedium for some, and apathy born of frustration for others, despite teachers' best efforts (when they occur) to mitigate it. It is simply a learned response.

All subjects are worth the same, grade-wise, time-wise, commitment-wise. Consider the apathy produced when a child who is desperate to sing or dance or draw is told that music or art happens once every two weeks, or these are simply eliminated from the curriculum entirely. It is another

---

2 The institutional forms of *not-listening* have their counterparts in a pattern of rebellion or resistance which the educator Herbert Kohl calls "not-learning": "Not-learning tends to take place when someone has to deal with unavoidable challenges to her or his personal and family loyalties, integrity, and identity. In such situations, there are forced choices and no apparent middle ground. To agree to learn from a stranger who does not respect your integrity causes a major loss of self. The only alternative is to not-learn and reject their world." *'I Won't Learn from You': And Other Thoughts on Creative Maladjustment.* New York, NY: New Press, 1994.

variety of *not-listening*, through which a child learns to devalue a core part of herself, and to disengage from it. And she learns to respond apathetically to that as well.

Or consider what happens when subjects are ruled by the watch or bell. Suppose the child found the morning's reading so engrossing that she wants to finish it after lunch, and is told she can't. What happens to a child's sense of coming to terms with what is important *for her* when every subject, every day, is allocated the same amount of time, and at precisely the same hour? Is this simply another instance of *not-listening* by design?

A form of call-and-response occurs in the classroom that passes itself off as a form of listening. Teachers (including and, maybe especially, those who are often considered to be good teachers) ask questions. Incessantly. It is almost a total bombardment, and essentially shields teachers from actually having to engage a child's own. A recent study (actually a reprise of an old one) placed graduate students in fifth grade classrooms across the country for several weeks. It was found that of all the questions ever asked, more than 90% of them were asked by teachers, and more than 90% of the time they already knew the answer. Rather than an expression of listening, or a way to engage active dialogue or to promote free inquiry, the questions are not really questions, but are intended as a kind of unrelenting, neverending test.

Consider how you would feel if you worked in an office environment five days a week, six hours a day, for 12 years, and your various bosses spent most of those six hours going from desk to desk, work station to work station, asking questions for which it was accepted that they already knew the answer. Would you feel strong, powerful, in control, creative, able to ask questions that would help you do your job better, in short, *enlarged*, or would you simply prefer to minimize the annoyance, or duck out when you saw the boss coming?

Those who respond to the battery in unacceptable ways can be treated. Our children can learn that their wholly natural responses mark themselves off as 'bad' children, and that this evil is built into their genes, and that they are ill, and that there are pills than can make them better, if the malady doesn't simply run its course like a bad case of mumps. For all the lip service we pay in our culture to valuing children, there is something wrong when we have come to view childhood as a disease in need of a diagnosis. Childhood is not a problem to be solved, or an illness to be cured, but the germ of power straining to be unleashed.

I could go on, but I think I've already made my point. Our methods of *education* (and I believe I am being charitable in calling them this) are designed to produce children, and future workers and citizens, who are apathetic, reduced, less than they could be, shrunken. It is a natural response when the wondrously messy process of learning is reduced to an institutional process of domestication, maintained the way it is for the purpose of making children more convenient to handle. If this was a book about politics, I would go on to illustrate what happens when the insensibility that Rabindranath Tagore escaped sets in, the political and economic uses of apathy, and plot out whose interests apathy serves, and whose are diminished. When you get me going on this, you'd quickly find out that I spare no quarters and take no prisoners either on what we have come to call the political Right or the Left. You'll have to wait for another book.

* * * * *

My interrogation was nothing but my yearning, and their response was nothing but their beauty.

— Augustine, *Confessiones,* Book X

And now, just when you thought it was safe to read on…a theological interlude. ("What is this man thinking? Isn't this supposed to be a homeschooling book?" "Oh, don't worry, he'll get there. Humor him a little: this is, after all, only the first chapter.")

In our preciously thin book of theology (it would be less than a page long, if we had one), Quakers subscribe, through experience or so we claim, to the notion that "there is that of God in each of us." This has applications for us in how we approach the world and, especially, the world of education. But what this expression truly means and, hence, its implications, are perhaps less clear than immediately meets the eye, and needs to be teased out.

One way of approaching this expression would be to say there is a "piece of God" in each of us. It would seem at one with the 18th Century deist (or even pantheist) beliefs held by many of the nation's Founding Fathers, men like Jefferson or Franklin (whose mother was a Friend) or Adams who, despite their individual differences, tended to look for the universal in that which united human beings. "All men are created equal," they would proclaim to the world, and despite both their use of the masculine noun or their divergence regarding African slaves, they looked forward to a time when this proclamation would be embodied both in personal behavior and political institutions.

For many (though by no means all) Friends, the expression takes on a rather simple (some would say simplistic) turn. If there is a piece of God in all human beings, how can one human being kill another? Conjoined with a no-nonsense interpretation of the Sermon on the Mount, and the first 300 years of early Christian history where it was understood to mean that all interpersonal violence, even in self-defense or in defense of one's family, is prohibited, Friends have tended to be pacifists. We are inclined, however, to take it one step further, as we cast doubt on the whole notion of enemies and adversaries, for to hate (or kill) another human being is to hate the God he holds inside him. Naïve, perhaps, but it has also opened up a way of thinking whereby we are called to look inside ourselves to see what commonalities we might hold with others, even those with practices and beliefs we think we might abhor.

A second way of viewing the idea that "there is that of God in each of us" is to subscribe to the conviction that Great Nature has placed something inside us that is sacred, and that partakes of the nature of the Divine. Not to get overly theological here (because we are not), we sometimes call it "the Seed", "the Light Within", "the Inward Teacher". It operates as, or something akin to, conscience, calling us to our higher selves if only we will heed it. We believe that, if given the chance, this seed guides us to what is "right", not necessarily through reason, but through a kind of dialogue between our temporal or situational setting, and that which transcends it. In a more narrow vein, it provides us with our feelings of guilt and shame—not negative emotions unless they are disabling, but leading us through action to a place in which we are at one with ourselves and the world. Since we have to come to experience that everyone has this seed, we assume the position that through dialogue we can each strive to bring forth each other's better natures.

But there is a third possible meaning and perhaps the most neglected. That which is "of God" in each of us is that which is unique, fundamentally different from that which inhabits every other being. Rather than that which is common to all of us, perhaps it is our kernel of identity, that which makes us who we are as individuals, which is "of God". We could envision it as each of us containing within ourselves a shard of a broken mirror, with all its jaggedness and sharp edges and erratic shape, none of which are meant to be sanded off or smoothed over, but which, when fitted together with all the other shapes in our mind's eye, give us a reflection, if but fleeting, of its creator. Or perhaps each is a different piece of tile in the Great Mosaic, and to buff out its color would mean for it to lose knowledge of its proper position in the whole. Or maybe we can imagine individual and distinct divine sparks having flown out from the Divine Center and, instead of running around as firemen trying to control or extinguish them as quickly as possible, we could think of it as our responsibility to provide fuel for the flame.

So what does this have to do with education? Well, perhaps from it, we can recognize a "right relationship" in learning with our children, and in so doing, with ourselves as well:

- Attend to that which you hold in common with your child, and with all children. When you see behaviors or learning patterns which you think are "difficult", think back upon the times that you might have exhibited the same, and you might better understand what is going on. The great Polish-Jewish educator Janusz Korczak once wrote about working with children, "First and foremost you must realize that you too are a child, whom you must first get to know, to bring up, and to educate."[3] If you feel you don't know yourself particularly well, you may be a little bit behind, but consider this your opportunity!

- Attend to dialogue, and, in doing so, call forth the deepest part of a child's sense of herself. Korczak again: "If we are constantly astonished at a child's perceptiveness, it means that we do not take them seriously." The quality of dialogue that a teacher or parent has with a child is critical, not because of what is said or taught and what is not, but because it and it alone can provide a model for the child's internal learning dialogue, that which she can only have with herself. John Holt, among the founders of contemporary homeschooling, once

---

3 Janusz Korczak, *A Voice for the Child: The Inspirational Words of Janusz Korczak*, edited by Sandra Joseph (London, UK: Thorsons, 1999). For a superb portrait of this extraordinary doctor, educator, and human being who collected and raised street children in Polish orphanages prior to World War II, and in a Jewish one inside the Warsaw Ghetto before he and all the children were exterminated, see Lifton, Betty Jean, *The King of Children: A Biography of Janusz Korczak* (New York, NY: Farrar, Straus & Giroux, 1988).

noted that what we learn from the best teachers is simply how to teach ourselves.

- When you find that which is unique in your child, or in anyone else you happen to meet, attend to it with the respect it deserves. For if it is truly that which is at her core, at the center, it has never been seen before and never will be again, neither upon the earth nor in the heavens. If you attend closely, she will teach you how to respond to it.

Attendance is mandatory, and we are taking roll.

Be. Be here. Be here now!

* * * * *

To watch the spirits of children, to nurture them in gospel love, and labor to help them against that which would mar the beauty of their minds, is a debt we owe them; and a faithful performance of our duty not only tends to their lasting benefit, and to our own peace, but also renders their company agreeable to us.

—John Woolman, "On Schools"

Love binds all things together.

Trust me—the subject matter isn't all that difficult. Oh, yes, you are worried about the mathematics, because by third grade you'd developed a phobia that you've never managed to shake. What about reading? Will he be hopelessly behind if he doesn't yet know all his vowel sounds? Does she really need that handwriting workbook? How is she going to do chemistry without a lab? And languages—do any of those computer programs really work?

If I can't help you out, you'll quickly find out that there is someone in the homeschooling community who can. There's well over a million of us now, united in our love for our children, from every race and ethnicity, economic class, family structure, religious persuasion, and educational philosophy, with a wide range of skills and experiences and resources that we are ready to share, most of the time for free! Chances are that, if you are asking about it, someone else has dealt with it before, and yet someone else is going to be coming to you for advice in a few years, so be prepared. There are more than a million experts out there, and you are going to be one of them!

The curriculum of love is not about externals. It is about what is essential in each individual human being, and in every child. Its watchwords are communication, inquisitiveness, acceptance, joy, honesty, courage, and, curiously, perhaps above all, intimacy. It demands that we minister to our children in their seeking to embrace a world that is their own, and prepared to render up her secrets. It is about surprises, unveilings, moments of spontaneous recognition, journeys completed and new ones waiting to be undertaken. It is about being at home—in oneself—and going home—to a larger world that awaits us all.

The curriculum of love is about you as much as it is about your child. It takes two to tango. Yes, you will be equipping her with skills and tools and knowledge and insights. You will be protecting her from dangers. But more than that, you will be creating a warm place in which will be housed that great treasure trove of memory, the place where her individual and unique identity will become—her. You will find yourself becoming, too, and coming home as well.

It's time to lay out the welcome mat.

* * * * *

I have a rather odd way of knowing when it is time for me to put out a new homeschooling book. It happens when I have a prepared keynote address ready for a homeschooling conference and find that, when delivering it, the digressions from the prepared text have become more interesting to me than the text itself. It means that my thinking is growing out of its old shell, and needs a new structure. Then it is just a matter of time to get it all down on the yellow pad and the computer (and make sure my long-suffering publisher is still interested! Thank you, Greg.)

This book consists of essays written since the publication of *Homeschooling and the Voyage of Self-Discovery: A Journey of Original Seeking* (Common Courage Press, 2003), though some have earlier roots. Some have been previously published in my "My Word!" column in *Home Education Magazine*, while others have appeared in *The Link* prior to the inception of my new regular column "What Really Matters", undertaken with Joyce Reed. Still others have appeared in *Life Learning Magazine, Home Educators Family Times*, and several online journals. While a few appear almost unchanged from their original publication, others have been edited or significantly expanded. Several have never appeared in print before.

As in my previous book, themes will be found to repeat within this volume. I have not attempted to edit out the repetitions, but rather to maintain the completeness of each individual essay. If you are a busy homeschooling parent, one essay per sitting might be the maximum for which you have time before duty, and love, call. So I have worked to ensure that each piece can stand on its own. For my cover-to-cover readers, let repetition be a sign of the intensity with which that particular tiger has me by the throat.

This book could have been written without help from anyone...but you wouldn't have wanted to read it. It would have been a very dull book, without the color of multiple experiences, and without the insights that only the combined wisdom of many can offer. Again I have drawn upon dialogues and feedback from various e-mail lists, most notably the Quaker Homeschooling Circle, to whose members I am especially grateful.[4] As I get older, the lengthening shadow reflects the long and growing list of people, places, institutions, organizations, and opportunities that made me and continue to remake me into whom I am. I categorically refuse to absolve any of them of responsibility for anything that is written here. On the contrary, if they find themselves indicted, I am willing to share. Honestly, that's just the way it is, and I thank them, and you, for helping to bear what I hope will not be found to be too weighty a burden.

---

4   If you are interested in checking out the Quaker Homeschooling Circle, you can find us at www.topica.com under our name. We welcome Friends and fellow travelers, homeschoolers and other seekers. For more information about Friends generally, you can find just about everything at www.quaker.org.

Unfinished Business

Freedom is not an ideal located outside of man; nor is it an idea which becomes myth. It is rather the indispensable condition for the quest for human completion.

— Paolo Freire

I am starting this essay as a way of putting off another piece of writing that I owe one of my publishers. It's not the first time this has happened. I can indeed write to order, but as a writer, I have learned that I can use my craft as a form of procrastination as well.

My hard drive is habitation to a cornucopia of essays, stories, book outlines, meditations, all in a half-finished state. Or even less. I'm hoping you'll get to see most of them eventually, but I wouldn't hold my breath.

Let me see. Here's one called "Attachment Everything", where I try to extend the idea of attachment parenting so that children can find themselves embraced by the world. Then there is "Learning from Ronco," on constructing an interesting, imaginative, integrated curriculum from watching infomercials (have any of you tried the "eggstractor" yet? Six months worth of physics in that little fabricated piece of plastic!) There's one christened "The Great Homonym", on principals and principles. Here's a little something on "Sacred Cows", which I think is about the wonders of foreign travel (but I'm not sure yet.) There's "Life is a Cabaret", about educational metaphors, with a bit of Charles Dickens thrown in for good measure. Thirty pages of notes on six- and seven-year-olds, and a short piece on kids playing baseball and the creation of meaning. More on perfectionism. There's a big, long thing, maybe even a book, on mentoring young teens and connecting them up in the community (a "how-to", it would likely sell too well, so it's probably not for me.) A couple of stories, a group of humorous stories tentatively titled "Wilderness Tales: New Yorker Meets the Natural World", and I'm still busy rewriting the Old Testament.

There are more. I'm thinking perhaps I can turn this into an extended "reality show", and invite readers of this book to vote for what you'd like me to try to finish next. At the very least, you're all invited to write to me, with the knowledge that as soon as I wrap one up, two more will pop up in its place.

Somewhere along the line I learned that there was a difference between something being completed, and it being finished. I know that sounds like some kind of Zen conundrum. But sometimes, while the product may be unfinished as far as anyone else viewing it might be concerned, the inner work demanded has been completed, and my presence is called upon to head off in another direction. Now and again I will force myself to put one word in front of the other (it's kind of funny that the last word should be the most recent in an author's mind), and maybe, just maybe, it will result in a royalty check. Other times it just goes back into the mental stew. And, though rarely, there are occasions when a piece of writing left behind like an abandoned shack, all of a sudden looks in my mind's eye like an hospitable cottage by the seashore, if I'll just fix the roof, hang the shingles, and plant some hydrangeas out front.

I often get agitated queries from homeschooling parents about their children never finishing *anything*. Of course know this isn't so—they likely finished that glass of milk they had for breakfast this morning, or the candy bars given them by the next-door neighbor. But the concern is that the kids are turning into quitters, and that there's never anything to show for the effort. The parents themselves feel invalidated as a result; there is a kind of Protestant ethic at work, and it is the parent who has sinned. There's the six-year-old who quits karate class after four months, or the violinist who insists on stopping the lessons or simply won't practice anymore, or the seeming mathwiz who will never finish the page in the workbook, or the artist who keeps ripping up his drawings before he will let anyone actually see them.

Sigh. I always ask parents to consider—just consider—that the work was completed, even if the course of study or the term's lessons aren't finished, or the workbook page not entirely filled in. After all, four months in the life of a six-year-old is the equivalent of *three years* in the span of a 40-year-old (even more, developmentally speaking), perhaps more than enough time to take in what feeds her body and soul at this juncture. It is not like the violin is about to disappear from the face of the earth, or grandma really needs to see sonny boy's use of the new coloring pens. And there will *always* be more math to do.

I am reminded rather viscerally of my mother who every night at dinnertime would fill my plate without consulting me as to how hungry I was, and then be upset if I didn't finish everything on it. Alternatively, on those rare occasions when I finished everything very quickly because

I wanted to go out and play, I'd be admonished not to "gobble my food", followed without a not-to-be challenged insistence that I must eat some more.

There is satisfaction to be gained from a job properly done, of course, from labors brought to fruition. If our own lives are going well, it is to be hoped that our children will witness this secondhand, and profit from the experience. They will learn soon enough that not everything is easy, and that moving themselves forward on their knowledge quests requires time, energy, and effort, and that it has to be their own. We are there to show them the field, give them the ball, help them learn the rules, find the right coach (ourselves or others), and stand on the sidelines and cheer. And we'll give them a big hug when the game is over, only to bring them out to practice the next week.

Finished products are like small islands in the uncompleted river of our lives. They are little waystations, places to pause and reflect and celebrate, bask in the joy of the moment, only to push off back into the center of the current again.

But it is our nature as human beings to be aware of our own incompleteness, and it is our inner sense of this lack of completion that sets us—and our children—striving, outward and upward in that great spiral dance we call living. It is not a lunge for the finish line—there will be plenty of opportunity later for someone else to write our obituaries, and we hope they will be kind. In the meanwhile, we have plenty of better things to do with our time.

Hey, gotta run. Break is definitely over. My daughter is calling me, and there's some unfinished business to attend to.

Stickers

The piano teacher had a shocked, even horrified, look on her face.

"Doesn't Meera (my younger daughter) like the stickers? All the other kids do."

"Of course she does. In fact, she has an entire collection of them at home." We'd had this discussion before with violin teachers for Aliyah—my older one, so we knew where this was headed.

"So why can't I give them to her?" The teacher now looked pained.

"Oh, do give them to her," my wife replied, "we don't object. But don't give them as a reward after she finishes and perfects a piece of music. Paste them on the page to mark where she is supposed to start a new one."

And she did.

For years, what would happen next became routine.

"It's too hard!" We would hear Meera's plaintive voice emanating from the living room.

We learned to butt out. We were meant to overhear, but this was a conversation Meera was having with the piano, and, progressively, with Grieg, Bach, Mozart, Gershwin, Granados, Beethoven, and Rachmaninoff, not with us. Twenty or 30 or 40 or 50 minutes later, or maybe even in two or three days, her playing of the new piece would be like breathing.

And somewhere along the line, and I don't remember when, the complaints disappeared. And so did the stickers.

* * * * *

There is an old expression, "Experience is its own reward." Of course, just because it is old, doesn't necessarily make it true, but in a world rife with uncertainty, and often fixated upon punishments and rewards, an attitude that enables one to find at least some satisfaction in the learning that comes with experience—academic or otherwise—might be worth cultivating. Or so seems reasonable to me.

The problem is, how do you learn that "experience is its own reward" unless you have had experience of it? The answer is you can't. And if you are always seeking external rewards, or avoiding punishments, it is easy for this learning to pass you by.

What to do? I think it might be worthwhile to take a page from other cultures and traditions. In many places in the Islamic world, a child is given

Meera in concert, Olympia, Washington, October, 2004.

dates in a sweet syrup before learning his first words from the Koran. In the Jewish tradition, children are given bread soaked in honey prior to reading their first words from the Torah. In fact, I have heard tell of at least one rabbi who places a drop of honey on each letter as children learn the Hebrew alphabet. They lick the honey off, and the letter is revealed.

When I lived in India, I witnessed a holiday that is celebrated every January/February called *Saraswati Puja* (simply, "Saraswati worship"). Saraswati being the goddess of memory, knowledge, and of music, children are brought to the temple on this day to learn their first letters, or to have their first music lesson under her blessing. Adults will also bring newly purchased tools of their trade—farmers with sickles, or tractors; accountants with computers; photographers with cameras—so that they may blessed with the knowledge to use them wisely. School children will bring new pencils, pens, erasers, empty notebooks, and unread textbooks and lay them at the foot of the altar, and cover them with flowers.

And there's more. Saraswati Puja is the one day each year that very young girls are allowed to wear *sarees* (clothing consisting of a wrapped piece of cloth, six meters long, normally reserved for adult women). It is a celebration of anticipation, an expression of the excitement—and the fulfillment—that is to come with the experience that lies ahead.

Translated literally, Saraswati means "the flowing one". She is the goddess of rivers, and hence of purification, but she also represents the flow of experience that is to come. The prayer to Saraswati expresses one's trust in her blessings without fear, the anticipatory knowledge that we will all some day 'grow into our *sarees*', into the people we are meant to be.

I guess all this amounts to for us in our day-to-day homeschooling practice is relatively simple: regardless of how you approach your children's education, be sure to provide them, continuously, a honeyed taste of the future that lies ahead with the knowledge yet to be attained. Read books to them that are currently beyond their own reading capabilities. Bring home videos from the library on scientific or mathematical topics they have yet to explore. Before starting geometry (if that's what you and they have decided to be doing), have your children go out and meet an architect. When learning about the Constitution, have them go to your local courthouse and watch the judicial system in action.

And when there is a subject you are sure they are really excited, really passionate, about, make sure they have at least one challenge in front of them that *you* think is just too hard! You never know....

The point is not whether they remember the information or are able to regurgitate it on demand, but that they are afforded the opportunity to develop an expanded sense of themselves, and an attitude toward the knowledge quest through which they are truly to be made whole.

And celebrate! Encountering the new and strange is an act of courage, and children are the bravest people in the world! You can help them along by celebrating their bravery. (This can be particularly helpful with children whose perfectionist tendencies are getting in the way of their embracing the journey.)

Mark new beginnings. Take your daughter to lunch before the first soccer practice. Come up with a family "fight song" to sing when beginning to learn carrying subtraction. Have little presents ready for all occasions—not just for graduations, but for commencements. Keep a family journal, and mark new initiatives. You will cherish it later. If you are a religious family, develop a prayer for inaugurating new directions, fresh unfoldings. These will take on their own rhythm, and will deepen in meaning for you and your family as the river of time passes you by, and you are washed in its sweetness.

* * * * *

Meera, now 12, put on her bathing suit, and shorts and a tee-shirt on top, and a pair of pink rubber flip-flops. She had been home from piano camp, held at Washington State University, for a week now. It was an unusually warm day.

"Dad, can you take me down to the fountain?" (Our town has a public fountain, an interesting sprinkler system that squirts water out of the ground and where hundreds of people go to cool off on a hot summer's day.)

"Sure," I replied, rescuing my sandals from underneath a panting, July-affected canine curled up by the foot of the couch.

On approaching the fountain, I quickly realized that this was a bad idea. There was a community fair happening only two blocks away, and parking looked like it was going to be impossible. I made my misgivings audible.

"Actually," suggested Meera casually, "could we go to the music store instead?"

Just then, not half a block from the fountain, a car pulled out directly in front of me.

"Are you sure?" I asked, seeing a parking space there for the asking.

"Yes, let's go to the music store."

Hijacked, I drove past the fountain (and the parking space!) and a mile up the hill to the music store.

We shuffled over to the music racks.

"That one," she pointed, with just a hint of hesitation.

Alexander Scriabin—Complete Etudes.

"Why that one?" I gulped, but trying to sound as nonchalant as I could.

"Everyone at camp said they are too hard, and no one would try them."

I handed her the book. She took it over to one of the practice pianos and started to play.

"So?" I asked.

Meera smiled. "Can you get it for me?"

More of the family jewels left at the music store. Home we went. Meera sits down at the piano and does a little "sampling", three or four or six bars of each (there are 26 etudes, each seemingly progressively more difficult), and then puts on her helmet, climbs on her bicycle, and races down the driveway to play with her ten-year-old friend at the end of the cul de sac. I'm used to this routine—it could take days or even a couple of weeks before she finally decides which piece she is going to try to master. Or, maybe, the book will just sit for a month or two (or four or five, except watching Meera's drive of late....) I have enough experience to know that sooner or later it will rise to the top of the pile again. Her teacher will gulp, too, but he won't say no.

During my lunch hour, I intend to take a trip downtown to a toy store located one block from the fountain and purchase a big purple Teddy Bear sticker.

It's going to get pasted on *Scriabin*.

(I'm a lucky guy!)

Just Do the Math!

N ot possible," homeschool mom proclaimed glumly, shaking her head.

I had just explained how the Sudbury Valley School (www.sudval.org), a democratically managed, child-directed learning environment that has been around for almost 40 years, has demonstrated repeatedly that a child could learn math—*all of it* grades K through 12—in eight weeks. Average (if there is such a thing), normal (never met one), healthy children, scores of them, learned it all, leading to admissions to some of the leading colleges and universities in the nation.

"Must be some kind of trick," she insisted dolefully, remembering her own dark days in the classroom slaving over the seemingly inscrutable, all joy wrung out as from a wet sponge, then as an elementary school teacher herself, and now finally fighting daily what she was convinced was a losing homeschooling war with her nine-year-old over the required workbook pages.

"Nope, no tricks, no special techniques, magic curriculum, or innovative teaching method," I informed her. The secret, if there was one, was to wait until the child asked for it, indeed insisted upon it, and could make use of it, even if the use was just college admission.

I directed her to an article on the Sudbury Valley website "And 'Rithmetic" (from the book *Free at Last*—www.sudval.org/05_onli_ 11.html). In it, the author and school co-founder Dan Greenberg writes of teaching a group of a dozen boys and girls, ages 9-12, the entire K-6 math portfolio in 20 contact hours. Greenberg, who admits sheepishly that in a past lifetime (in the 1960s) he was partially responsible for the development of the "new math" and now has lived long enough to regret it, tried to dissuade them by suggesting that it would be a lot more fun to go out and play. But no use—they were obstinate and determined. He set only one rule: be on time, 11 a.m. sharp, twice a week, for a half an hour. If anyone was five minutes late, class was cancelled. If it happened twice, no more teaching.

Greenberg found an old math primer published in 1898, with lots of exercises, and away they went. No shortcuts. They added the long columns and the short columns, the fat ones and skinny ones, "borrowed" and "carried" and memorized the times tables. Long division. Fractions. Decimals. Percentages. Square roots. [Square roots? They stopped teaching that in the '60s, I think (was Greenberg responsible?) The more "gifted" among us were given sliderules.]

In 20 contact hours, every single one of the kids knew the material cold. No slackers. No failures. No one "left back". No "math anxiety". No boredom, frustration, embarrassment. No shame or humiliation. No competition, "achievement", "failure", or "success". No prizes. Just 'rithmetic. The students held a party to celebrate.

Walking around in a self-congratulatory haze, Greenberg contacted a friend, a leading elementary math specialist in the public schools, to gloat.

"Not surprising," mused his friend.

"Why not," asked Greenberg, having had the wind at least temporarily removed from his sails.

"Because everyone knows," he replied, verbally stomping on Greenberg's ego, "that the subject matter itself isn't all that hard. What's hard, virtually impossible, is beating it into the heads of youngsters who hate every step. The only way we have a ghost of a chance is to hammer away at the stuff bit by bit every day for years. Even then it does not work." (Honesty is refreshing, isn't it?) "Most of the sixth graders are mathematical illiterates. Give me a kid who wants to learn the stuff—well, 20 hours or so makes sense."

I could see homeschool mom becoming more disconsolate by the minute. She could begin to get her head around it, maybe, for the K-6 stuff, but what about all that algebra and geometry and trigonometry and pre-calculus? (Whatever that is—when I was in school, it didn't exist—is it some kind of holding pen?) I asked her if she remembered learning much at times when she herself was unmotivated, uncommitted, and uninspired. I felt like apologizing the moment I asked, for it was the wrong question, as all I had succeeded in doing was to make her feel *uncomfortable*.

"Try this," I suggested, "Let's do the math together. Let's imagine you were one of those kids who, as a teen, was really motivated, ready to spend 30 hours a weeks on getting all the math down. (I used the 30-hour figure because it is about the number of hours per week the "average" high school kid *spends* in the classroom. I like the metaphorical "spending" as it begs the question as to what is being given in exchange.) And then, let's compare what might happen if you were to learn the same stuff in school."

Now studies have shown that in the standard U.S. school day at the average American public school, approximately one hour and 15 minutes goes into actual instruction of new material. That's right—75 minutes. This is not as strange as it might initially sound. Consider what happens in a six-hour school day: movement from class-to-class and the required settling in and getting up, attendance-taking, pledge, bureaucratic busywork, lunch, recess, "physical education", drug-taking (both of the prescribed and illicit variety), sexual harassment. Inside the classroom, review of stuff from the day before, last week, or last year; homework assignments collection and distribution; dealing with "behavior problems"; classroom organization; tests, including review time for the statewide ones—you get the picture. I'm ignoring the days the student is sick, or the teacher is sick, or the school is sick (lots of school buildings in my state get closed occasionally because of "Sick Building Syndrome"—I would have called schools "sick buildings" by definition, but let's not go there.)

So 75 minutes of new instruction time. But wait! Since instruction is aimed at the "average" kid, 50 percent of the time the student already knows what is being taught, so the actual instruction time *from the child's perspective* is closer to 40 minutes a day. Now let us imagine that 40 percent of that, or 15 minutes a day, is devoted to math. (But wait again! A good portion of that time while the child is being instructed, she would prefer to be somewhere—anywhere—else!)

Anyhow, do the math: 15 minutes a day, 75 minutes a week, for a 180-day school year comes to 2,700 minutes or 45 hours per school year (of which a portion is in time during which the child wasn't paying attention, or just didn't want to learn—so figure 30 hours a year.) But wait again! Some of that formal math in the early years was being taught at a time when it took twice or three times as long as it would have later. After all, Greenberg had already demonstrated that all of K-6 required only 20 contact hours.

So, do the math. If you figure the actual math time at 30 hours a year for 8 years (accounting for the wasted time in the early years), it totals 240 hours. Lo and behold—if, at age 15 or so, you *wanted* to learn all the math K-12, weren't inhibited by math anxiety, and were willing to spend 30 hours a week at it, it would take you...8 weeks!

Nothing magic here, except that you might actually learn it.

If you never teach a stitch of math, in a mathematical culture your kids will learn heaps of it anyway. Whether it be from reckoning time/distance/velocity ratios so they can figure out how soon they'll get home from looking at highway signs, to ascertaining how many Twinkies they can get with their allowance (Twinkies? Does that date me?), to helping dad bake the pies or mom replace the oil in the car (How many quarts is that? Why are engines measured in liters?), learning math along the journey is a difficult thing to avoid.

Want a place to start? If your son has a sweet tooth, play "The Cost is Right". Go to the supermarket, and give him two bucks. Tell him he can buy as much candy as he can manage with $2 (no tax at this stage), but that if the total adds up to more than two smackers, he loses it all. You'll be amazed at how swiftly the two-place, long-list, carrying addition falls into place, and the multiplication, and the borrowing subtraction. If you watch carefully, you'll also discover something really interesting: the "correct" way to add a group of multi-place numbers is from left to right, not right to left, and anyone who has $2.50 in his pocket and needs to buy a can of cream-style corn (88¢) and a bag of kidney beans ($1.39) knows it. That's why you had to spend all that time on those horrible worksheets, to train you in a method that goes against the grain of all human experience! (Nothing wrong with that, and it's nice to have an 'alternative' method at your disposal.) Got two competitive kids? Really play "The Cost is Right," and the winner gets an extra dollar for next time.

Have your daughter help you fill up the car with gas (and appoint her as the lookout for fluctuating prices in the neighborhood.) Let her make the change, and compute your gas mileage. On a long trip, deputize her to count the number of trucks you pass on the highway (I'm assuming you speed like the rest of us), and figure out how many you pass per hour, or per 100 miles.

Daughter saving her allowance and birthday presents to purchase the poodle? Paste a picture of Mr. Poodle on top of a bar graph and make plotting out progress toward the goal part of the exercise. Get a special poodle-purchase bank account. (In better times, you might even get to explain interest, but currently there isn't likely to be any.)

Petey the Poodle Puppy already arrived? Well, put some graph paper on the wall, and make weighing and measuring part of caring for said canine. (Speaking from personal experience, I can tell you it works for snakes as well.) Say, every two weeks. Height, length, maybe even girth, too. Think of it as future veterinarian training. Put two graphs on the wall, and measure the "child puppy" as well. (Most children love to see analogies to their own development.) You might decide to do the same with dad, but only if he's on Atkins.

You get the idea. If you still feel your child MUST do the workbook thing, so be it. But remember that whether she succeeds with it or not will be more a function of motivation and inspiration than anything else. Give her a reason and a purpose that becomes her own and she will discover an education truly worthy of the name.

(Might take even less than eight weeks.)

* * * * *

San Diego homeschooling mom Julie Brennan, a CPA who was formerly employed by two international public accounting and consulting firms, has created an awesome website called "Living Math!" She has been working to find ways to link math to real settings, and to the human drama—the history and literature—that created mathematics as we know it. Julie has developed a family math group, set up a discussion forum related to living math methods and materials (great archives!), and a 'heart of mathematics' study group. There are terrific book reviews, and an enormous number of resources and book recommendations and links. You can wallow in it for days! Check it out at www.livingmath.net

Joy

Joy to the world
All you boys and girls
Joy to the fishes in the deep blue sea
Joy to you and me.

—Three Dog Night

I just returned from my first (ever!) orchestra rehearsal. A friend of mine (a bass clarinet player) invited me, assuring me that the music wouldn't be too hard, the conductor was a middle-school band teacher, and the community orchestra was desperate for violins (and those with pretensions of playing them.)

"Do I have to get the music in advance," I inquired, probably with a little edge to my voice.

"No," she said, "Just show up."

I did. I learned a long time ago that just showing up is about 90% of the game. Having just past my 53rd birthday, I took the invitation as one of those now-or-never opportunities.

I found a perch way up in the back of the room, forming my own last row of violins. There was Purcell! And Weber!! And Brahms!!! And Massenet!!!! And Tschaikovsky!!!!! Woo-hoo!!!!!!

"So, how'd it go," asked my daughter Aliyah on my return home.

"Well," I replied, in a rather neutral tone of voice, "I couldn't follow the conductor. I had trouble counting. I could barely play the music, and some of it I couldn't play at all. I had difficulties *reading* the music. I couldn't get my bow to go in the same direction as the section leader's. I couldn't hear myself playing, and I couldn't hear anyone else playing either."

"Oh," she said, with a look of commiseration on her face, she having played in orchestras since she was eight.

"But, actually," I added, smiling, "I did just fine."

* * * * *

Did, too. Oh, I know. There were "problems". But they'll get fixed, one at a time. And some of them, well, maybe they won't. Those are the breaks. There are no Yehudi Menuhins in this small-town community orchestra, and I'm not about to break the pattern. And, though I am a little sheepish to admit it, I was relieved to discover there is a cellist who is far more musically out to lunch than I am.

People who know me often comment on my somewhat expansive list of avocations, and the fact that they are rather disparate in nature. I fiddle, and I sing opera (had my operatic debut, together with my daughter, last summer in *The Magic Flute,* and will be singing in *Carmen* this spring (though they wouldn't let me try out for the part of the bull). I write and tell stories (and just published two books on the uses of storytelling), and have been threatening to rewrite the Old Testament so that it is more to my liking (I've actually started—you can e-mail me for samples.) I read voraciously in social and, especially, Quaker history. I have a passion for things Asian Indian—art, music, philosophy, culture, food, and play a south Indian musical instrument, the *veena*. I like to cook. I've become a bit of a stargazer (saw Saturn "in the flesh" for the first time on October 31, 1996, at the age of 46.) Oil painting, sculpture, stained glass window-making are looming somewhere over future horizons.

I have some "natural" affinity in a few of these areas (my opera singing really is pretty good!), and some, like violin-playing, ah-hem, I try reasonably hard, and among the second violins, I can fake it pretty well. But they all give me joy!

What do these all have in common? I'm sitting here, scratching my head. And then it became obvious. I didn't study and didn't even have "exposure" to any of these activities in public school!

Isn't that strange? Now I wasn't a particularly unhappy camper in school. I got all "A"s, in absolutely everything (except phys. ed.). An honor student! Teachers and school administrators liked having me around. I was a "success" story and added to *their* reputations. Why, I'm not quite sure.

But, somehow, virtually everything I studied in school had the joy leached out of it, and, sooner rather than later, became toxic. I seemed to have some natural talents in math and science, or so I was told. And, at the time, I thought I loved mathematics, because I was taught that I was good at it.

My teachers—good or bad, I'm not even sure I know now which were which—seemed determined to make sure I always got the "right" answers. And I did, which pleased them greatly. The point wasn't to enable me or even allow me to ask interesting questions. In fact, at that point of my life, I never imagined that there even were such things as interesting questions when it came to mathematics. I simply received rewards for right answers. The environment was well policed to ensure all was accomplished in the required manner. "You need to be able to explain how you got the answer," they insisted, and a non-response or the suggestion that it had been whispered in my ear by the Jolly Green Giant would have been grounds for "corrective action". There were good cops and bad cops, those I liked and those I didn't, but looking back, it doesn't seem to me that the type of math cop made much difference. When the compulsory ordeal was over, I had no reason why I would want to look at a math problem ever again (after all, there were no more rewards), and all it would remind me of was the nature of my past incarceration. I met many a math teacher, but I never met a mathematician until I was 25, and the idea that one could actually take delight in a mathematical journey seemed like heresy in a world obsessed with "right" answers. As for its potential utility in my life, spending six weeks in learning how to use a sliderule pretty much sums it up.

Science was no better. I was a star! I was quick with facts, and careful with beakers. We all did our "experiments", making sure to end up with the predetermined result. If the results differed from that which was expected, it must have been a mistake, rather like baking a cake that didn't rise. The only "experiment" was to find out whether we could make the results conform. Otherwise, we would dispose of the various materials as best we could, pour the chemicals down the sink, and start again. Conformity, I quickly learned, was the cornerstone of the scientific method. Compulsory canned experiments, compulsory canned results, and woe to the student who wanted to start with a different hypothesis! So much for scientific inquiry, although maybe the experiment had to do with me—"How high a grade can we give him in science without him ever asking a single, meaningful scientific question?"

I could go on, but I think you get the point. Nowhere in any of this was there even the hint of recognition that this was *my* education.

I've spent a good part of the past 30 years in recovery. Learning to find joy in doing things at which I may or may not be particularly adept is part of the required discipline, and it's working. You'll notice that all those visual arts activities are still in the offing. I grew up with the double whammy of being told rather explicitly that I wasn't any good with crayons, coupled with the sense that drawing or painting or playing with clay wasn't of much value anyway. "Works of art" were simply objects that existed in museums, and never mind how they were created. The whole idea that I might choose to engage in such activities because they might provide some inner satisfaction never seems to have crossed anyone's mind, or at least it wasn't conveyed to me. I promise to write about the results when I get to that part of my journey.

In the meantime, there are my kids. Dad is now a source of great amusement, even if he is occasionally, well, *embarrassing*. I hope I am modeling for how they will be around *my* grandkids. And, let me inform them now: sooner or later, they are going to inherit the paintings. (I think that means I have just made a commitment.)

The Frontier Spirit of the Heart

Harry Potter just doesn't do it for me.

I don't mean to be a spoilsport. Perhaps I am "imaginatively challenged", in which case I ask your pardon for my infirmity. We own all the available volumes, though none were purchased at the stroke of midnight on release day. Both my daughters read them, with varying degrees of enjoyment. (On the whole, with my kids, Harry is batting one for two.) My wife spent two days usurping the dog's place on the couch over the weekend until the most recent volume was consumed. Me? I never get past the first 20 pages.

I've no particular objections, though. The good guys always win, or so I've been told. Blood and gore are severely limited. Sex doesn't seem to have crossed anyone's mind, or at least not very often, which seems somewhat surprising (and truly a fantasy), given that, after all, the story takes place in an English boarding school. Drugs are transformed into potions, and haven't seemed to inspire any pharmacologically crazed raves lately. Dress, is, shall we say, decidedly conservative? For kids forced to undergo the dreary shower in our nation's educational gas chambers (the air quality in some 20% of U.S. schools not meeting E.P.A. indoor air quality standards *for adults*), the hocus pocus at least holds out small hopes of freedom, and that's no mean feat. No wonder it gets some of the nation's school-incarcerated children to read for the first time—*Harry Potter* is the preteen equivalent of "liberation theology". And our homeschooled ones can well feel it when their peers are picking up on a good thing.

But, decidedly earthbound as I appear to be, as well as being a writer myself, I am more than a little intrigued by the story of the author. Best I can make out, here is the story of a single mom on welfare who spent more than a decade avoiding 'earning a living'. J.K. Rowling went to college to study French, with her parents hoping she'd become a bilingual secretary. She describes herself as having been "the worst secretary ever"—she couldn't remain attentive during meetings, and wrote down story ideas rather than taking notes. Needless to say, her "career" didn't last all that long. She moved to Portugal, worked part-time as an English teacher, got married, gave birth to a daughter, and promptly got divorced.

Rowling then moved to Edinburgh, Scotland, where she could sponge off her younger sister, settle into the British equivalent of public housing, and live off the dole. She did her writing in an inexpensive restaurant co-owned by her brother-in-law, where she took her daughter so that she wouldn't have to pay for heat, and solicited and received a small grant from the government in order to complete her manuscript. Up until the first book of *Harry*, she hadn't published a darn thing.

Now, it is reported that Ms. Rowling's personal fortune is greater than that of the Queen of England, which I find perfectly and serendipitously delightful. (The last time I looked, the Queen was still on public assistance.) From the interviews I've seen on television, Rowling seems like a pretty nice lady, and I guess it is hard to complain when nice people end up with money, with the caveat of a hope that it doesn't *change* them.

And that's just the thing: J. K. Rowling was the same person before and after we were introduced to Harry. Her writing was the same, both before and after she became exceedingly rich from it. And, having once turned in her manuscript, she had almost no role in *Harry*'s success. Chalk that one up to a good agent, and I wish he were working for me!

So this raises a beguiling question, and one I think worthy for homeschooling parents to grapple with. Was J.K. Rowling any less a "success" while she was a welfare mom? If she were our kid, would we have preferred she go out and get a *real* job, instead of scribbling away like she did when she was 6? Even consider her writing—was it any less good sitting unpublished on the table in Nicholson's Cafe, or would it have had any less quality had it been published by any of thousands of tiny English or American publishers, and, for lack of good promotion, died a quiet death, never having made the slightest ripple in the publishing world?

What do we teach our children about how to measure their own success? Or our own? Wouldn't you like to read an interview with J.K. Rowling's father? (Her mother died long ago.) Would it be little more than "we knew all along she had it in her?" Or how "we clearly did the right thing for her, and steered her in the proper direction, for her training as a bilingual secretary has stood her in good stead?" When Harry started speaking to Joanne a decade before the publication of the first volume, should her parents have insisted she visit a psychiatrist, and made sure she was taking her meds?

What I appreciate most about the J.K. Rowling story is not so much her "stick-to-itiveness" (though I think there is a moral to be found there, too) as much as her commitment to carve out for herself a little zone of freedom, one which she could inhabit until Harry had completed at least the first stage of his education. It may have been rather sparse in creature comforts (unheated Edinburgh flats can be mighty cold in *summer*, let alone when the days turn gnarly.) I imagine this freedom carried with it its own cup of loneliness, only partially mitigated by the sometimes joyous, sometimes annoying tugs of Harry pulling at her heartstrings.

There was a time in history when people journeyed physically into the unknown. There was a frontier spirit that explored and settled the American West, and a frontier spirit that led climbers up Mount Everest. Now, of course, the Grand Canyon is choked with air pollution, and Yellowstone littered with snowmobiles. African elephants are caught between various warring factions, and an ascent of Everest requires reservations years in advance.

But there is still a frontier spirit of the heart. All of our kids are born with at least a little of it. It is what equips them with the courage to take their first halting steps, to attempt to tie their shoes, to make out their first letters in the jumble of signs, to get on their bicycles and peddle down the alleyway, to paint their first picture, or craft their first story or poem. Needless to say, we all have our little tricks and techniques to help them along when we choose.

But, in doing so, do we take enough heed to allow them to find their own frontier of the spirit? Are we circumspect enough to avoid timetables, and to provide the space—the hours, weeks, years, or decades—to enable this spirit to take root firm and deep in that unique soil that is both its source and its destiny? Can we protect our children from society's well-meaning invasiveness, and our own?

Will we be prepared when we discover the tabby cat sitting on the garden wall next to the driveway, and the large, tawny owl fluttering by the window? What will our response be when the first letter arrives, addressed to the occupant of the cupboard under the stairs?

Shoelaces

After a lengthy investigation, a mathematician from Victoria, Australia reported in the journal *Nature* (Vol. 420, 2002) that there are approximately four hundred million different "reasonable" ways of tying a shoe with seven eyelets down each side. But, said Professor Burkard Polster of Monash University, "Hundreds of years of trial and error have led to the strongest way of lacing our shoes—the 'straight-lace' and 'criss-cross' methods." These two methods, it was found, provide the maximum horizontal tension on both sides of the shoe.

Polster's 40-page examination discovered that even slight variations could offset the results. For example, relative to the amount of lace used, the criss-cross method is slightly stronger than straight-lacing when eyelets are close together. The opposite is true when eyelets are further apart.

The differences resulting from shoe-tying are far more variable. Granny knots, whether single or double, are "notoriously unstable", noted Polster.

Whether Polster was wearing lace-up shoes or penny loafers when his findings were first reported to the media (December 10, 2002) is unknown.

* * * * *

Joey took a seat in the back of his kindergarten class, and was very pre-occupied.* The night before, for the very first time, and after weeks of trying, he had successfully managed to lace up and tie his own shoes. He had been so proud when he ran into the kitchen and danced before his mother, who promptly gave him a big hug and a kiss.

It had been a struggle. Weeks earlier, he had unlaced his shoes, and then, having forgotten entirely how they were supposed to look after they were laced back up again, gave up after a few half-hearted attempts. How clumsy his fingers felt in trying to aim that fat shoelace end through that little hole! And, so, distracted by something else less frustrating (and, hence, more interesting), he left the struggle behind.

Until it was time to go. Mom was in a rush.

"Joey, where are your shoes?" asked Mom accusingly, already knowing that, because of Joey (rather than her own poor planning), they were going to be late *as usual*.

---

* This story is based on an actual event that is reported to have occurred in Colorado in 2003.

"Uh, in my room?" Joey responded weakly, the inflection of his voice rising.

"Well, get them!" snapped his mother, in the verbal equivalent of stamping her feet.

Joey went to his room, and got his shoes.

"Where are the laces?" asked Mom accusingly (again).

"I...I don't know?" replied Joey, inflection still rising.

"What do you mean you don't know?"

His mother didn't wait for a reply.

"What a mess this is, Joey!" his mother proclaimed upon going into his room, supposedly for his benefit. "Didn't I tell you that you have to put things away after you use them?" she continued gratuitously, vaguely remembering her resolution to provide more shelf space, or at least some milk crates for Joey to put his stuff in.

She found the shoelaces between Eeyore and a pair of dirty socks that hadn't made it to the hamper.

"Joey, come in here right now!" the voice of authority rang out. "How many times do you have to be told that dirty socks have to go into the laundry?"

Joey handed his mother the shoes. She hurriedly put the laces back in, and told him to quickly put his shoes on. Of course, in his hurry, Joey paired the right shoe with the left foot, and the left shoe with the right foot (why couldn't they just be the same for both feet? Joey wondered.)

"Oh, give them here," spit his mother through her teeth, seething. She bent down, and forced the shoes onto the correct feet, and tied them, much too tight!!!

"Now, get in the car," she huffed, "and put on your seatbelt."

Off they went, first on an especially trying shopping expedition, and then to his friend's house. Joey's mother explained to his friend's mother why they were late, glaring at Joey as he played the whole time, and noting that this was the third time she had found Joey's shoes without the laces in them.

"Maybe he wants to learn how to tie his shoes himself," suggested his friend's mother. (Joey overheard, but didn't say anything.)

That evening, after dinner, his mother came into the room where Joey was playing with Tigger and Piglet and apologized, and asked whether Joey wanted to learn how to tie his own shoes. Joey nodded his head ever-so-slightly. And so they started.

"Over and under," said his mother, "like this." But something was wrong, his mother finally noted after about four days of abortive attempts. The shoe was sitting on Joey's little desk. But Joey kept looking down at his bare feet.

"Joey, today let's try it with the shoes already on your feet. Joey nodded, and sat down on the linoleum and put his shoes on.

"Now make the little rabbit ears," urged his mom, and Joey did, but the first part of the knot got loose. Slowly but surely, however, he gained confidence, and, one day, he spent the whole afternoon after school alone in his room, tying and untying his shoes until, finally, FINALLY, he did it! He couldn't wait to get to school the next day to show Mrs. Fieldston!

* * * * *

Mrs. Fieldston noticed that Joey had taken a seat in the back, which was very unusual for him, as he usually sat near the front so that, with his glasses and all, he could see better. For the better part of the first hour she saw his head virtually vanish behind the chairs in front of him, and then bob up and down, even as the other kids listened to her stories, and identified the letters on the blackboard. Not once did Joey raise his hand.

Finally, when the class took a break, she noticed that Joey had taken his shoes off and had to put them back on before going out in the hall, and was the last child to leave the room.

When class began again, Mrs. Fieldston took a peek behind the other kids' chairs after Joey's head had disappeared and saw that he had his shoes off again. All during math, she could see his head bobbing up and down, and not once did he volunteer to write a number on the board.

Finally, she could stand it no longer. While the other children were using their oversized pencils to copy the letters of the alphabet onto the wide-lined paper, Mrs. Fieldston walked back to her desk, opened the top left-hand drawer, and drew out a roll of silver duct tape.

She walked slowly and silently back to his place. Joey didn't even see her coming. She could see that he now had his shoes on, though they were untied. Mrs. Fieldston now towered over Joey. Without a word, she bent down, and proceeded to tape Joey's feet—over his socks—into his shoes. Then, with a large ripping sound, she tore off two more pieces of the duct tape and pressed them directly on top of the untied laces so that Joey could no longer get at them. Then, just as slowly and silently, she walked back to the front of the room, replaced the tape in the top left-hand drawer, closed the drawer and sat down, all the while watching the other kids drawing their letters.

"That will teach him," she thought.

The Greatest

All right. I admit it. I'm prejudiced. Perhaps the prejudices are ill-founded, but I seem to hang on to them anyway.

I don't like country music.

Now you have to understand, having grown up in New York City, my version of the "country" was a set of Catskill Mountain hotels, guaranteed to click my hayfever into high gear. The closest I ever came to cowboy entertainers was Rodney Dangerfield (bless his soul), the only corralling I'd ever witnessed was the ushering of elderly guests into a kosher hotel dining room.

But then there are the songs themselves. Too much cheatin' and beatin', lovin' and losin' for me to relate to—they simply aren't a reflection of my family values. Lonesome range riders, lithesome cowgirls, large pickup trucks, rifles and shotguns with pet names are just not part of my vocabulary. I apologize for my cultural blindness, and will strive to do better.

But when I came across Kenny Rogers' song "The Greatest", it was with a shock of recognition and, even, perhaps, an appropriate subject for a homeschooling essay.

In case you haven't heard it, the story of the song is about a little boy in a baseball hat standing alone in the middle of a field with his ball and bat. Time and again, he tosses the ball up in the air and takes a mighty swing. Each time, the ball falls harmlessly to the ground, and boy repeats out loud, "I am the greatest there has ever been," grits his teeth and tries again. Finally, his mother calls him into dinner, and so one last time the ball goes up, the bat is swung, the ball falls down, with the boy smiling to himself, saying:

> *"I am the greatest, that is understood,*
> *But even I didn't know I could pitch that good."*

In his mind, the boy had pitched a perfect game.

So much of the way we as children, and later as adults, go about building our lives has not so much to do with the skills and tools and experiences we pick up along the journey, but the way we go about infusing them with meaning. Sometimes, as I am all-too-aware when I am not "being all I can be" with my children, I discover how much my insistence on my own goals and objectives for a learning activity can get in the way of what is really important in my daughters' understanding of what they need to grow.

I spoke recently with a father who was very proud of having taught his seven-and-a-half year old to play a wicked game of chess. But having done so, he was extremely disappointed to find out that his son didn't want to play with him. Upon artful inquiry from his mother, the boy admitted that the real problem was that he didn't like the possibility (perhaps unlikely) that he might actually beat his father (which he thought would make his father feel bad), and that he didn't like doing battle against "good guys". He and his five-year-old sister preferred a "chess" game they had invented where together they competed against an army of ogres. Finally, when he'd ask his dad questions about knights and bishops, and why queens were so powerful in battle (all things that really interested him), his father told him to be quiet and concentrate.

I remember years ago taking my older daughter Aliyah, then age 5, to her first play, Gilbert and Sullivan's *The Pirates of Penzance*, performed by a group of kids. It was well-acted and well-sung, the music was terrific, and the pirate costumes were dashing. I hoped that this would lead to more dad-daughter theatrical outings, and it did, but I learned quickly that what had grabbed Aliyah was neither the story, nor the acting, nor the singing, nor the costumes. During the playing of the overture, a cardboard cat, mounted on a dowel, chased several dowel-mounted cardboard mice from stern-to-bow of a cardboard pirate ship, with similarly dowel-mounted cardboard seagulls flapping overhead. While my wife and I went to bed, apparently Aliyah did not, for in the morning we found that she had drawn and cut out entire casts of characters, raided the kitchen drawers for all the available chopsticks, and Scotch-taped the characters to them. The most important lesson she had picked up that evening was in art, something that had never even crossed my mind.

I met a mother with a nine-year-old daughter whose sole interest in life seemed to be horses. (All right, I have met dozens of mothers with similarly equine-smitten, XX-chromosomed offspring, but this one had a real story to tell.) The daughter hoped someday for a career in breeding them (they were fortunate enough to actually live in horse-breeding country), and had read every book she could find on the subject. But she told her mother that all of the books she had read seemed to refer back to one book, the bible of horse-breeding books as it were, and, it now having been translated from the French, she desperately wanted a copy. Expensive! Grandparents kicked in, and she received it as a Christmas present.

Several months later, her mother asked about the book. Was it better than the others? Well, no, actually, some of the others were more clearly written. Did it have better pictures than the other books? No, the photos were all in black-and-white, whereas some of the others had beautiful color photography. Was the information more complete? Actually, no, the book was even older than some of the others, and didn't have the most up-to-date information on certain breeds.

Her mother was puzzled by all of this, until she noticed one thing. Whenever her daughter went to visit a horse farm, or an equestrian event, she always carried this particular book under her arm. Not the one with the color pictures or the more up-to-date information or the clearest writing. This one. The book had become a talisman for her daughter, a symbol to her and for others that she was really serious about horses, and the future she saw in store for herself, and this particular book was a way of announcing it to the world.

Sometimes when we take our eye off the ball, and get too invested in whether our kids are learning *our* p's and q's, we can lose sight of the game—*their game*—and the investment they are willing to make in it if just given the chance. When all is said and done (and it never is, of course), this is *their* education, not ours, though it is gratifying (and sometimes breathtaking) to be taken along for the ride.

I remember, and it was a long time ago, when I received my one and only lesson in 'carpentry'. I was given a board that had already been used by others, and in which scores of bent nails remained, and was told to hammer my dozen into what could only best be described as the nail graveyard. I did my duty, none of the nails passing particularly straight, and handed the hammer along to the next child. And that, as best I can remember, was my lesson, in the days before liability concerns ruled the classroom, and hammering banished from the state's mandated learning objectives. How much more my hammering might have represented, and how much better my carpentry skills would be today, if I had been allowed the space to imagine the birdhouse, and the chicks inside, and the bluebird sitting on the peak of the nailed-together roof, singing.

Carmenizing

In the morning, I gave the keynote address at the annual Washington Homeschool Organization Convention. I put up a sign in the back of my book-signing booth. "Leaving at 4:00 p.m. Singing an Opera in Hoquiam. (Really!)"

It was a busy day. Up at 6 a.m. to get to Puyallup (I'm not even going to begin to try to help those of you unfamiliar with the place to pronounce it properly), pack up my wares, jump in the car, drive through Olympia, pick up older daughter who was selling her sculptures and jewelry at a local fair, and speed (guilty as charged) another hour-and-a-half to this small coastal community, change into costume (gypsies don't have to be too precise), throw on some makeup (mascara takes care of the gray in my moustache and I am young again!), and be on stage for the 7:30 curtain. I'm still recovering.

It had never been one of my life goals to sing opera. In fact, I can truthfully say it had never really crossed my mind until less than a year ago. I have been an intermittent opera lover for more than 30 years, but the closest I had ever come to actually being part of one was when I'd threaten the kids that if they didn't clean their rooms, I'd sing the high coloratura soprano aria from *Norma* at full volume. (Hint: it always did the trick, but you'll have to invite me to your home until I can figure out how to market the CD.)

I happened upon the new opera company by accident (or perhaps it was part of some higher plan). A flyer announced the need for choristers for Mozart's *The Magic Flute*, and Aliyah desperately wanted to sing. Knowing (or at least imagining) that it was unlikely a new opera company was going to take a flyer on a 14-year-old (however experienced a singer she happened to be), and also aware of the great shortage of male singers in most communities (let alone those interested in singing Mozart!) we figured to offer ourselves as a package deal. It worked! And instead of having to drive Aliyah to and from interminable rehearsals at all hours of the day, night, and weekends, I was already there!

To call our semi-professional company "Opera Pacifica" (www. operapacifica.com) a labor of love is an understatement. It was founded by two local aficionados whose paths to each other, and to us, could hardly be more unusual.

Claudia, the music director and conductor, now in her 50s, grew up

Aliyah (as gypsy) and David (as townsman) in Opera Pacifica's production of Carmen, June 2003.

in rural Georgia. By the age of 10, she could play the piano, pipe organ, clarinet, oboe, and baritone ukulele. She moved to Las Vegas where she became part of a successful nightclub act that toured the U.S., Canada, and the Bahamas. When the act went out on the road, they quickly realized they could save money if they had their own airplane pilot. Claudia volunteered, and logged thousands of hours in the air, so many, in fact, that she became one of the first three women hired by Continental Airlines to fly 727s. But the opera bug had bitten her early, and when she retired from Southwest Airlines in 1997, she spent the next five years in training as an opera conductor, including a stint with the National Opera Orchestra in Beijing. Now she rushes downs to conduct rehearsals from having spent the day training pilots on a flight simulator.

Bob, the vocal director and tenor soloist, grew up about three miles from me in New York City. Having joined the military after high school, he ended up in the (supposedly non-existent, but very real) CIA operation in Laos during the Viet Nam War, for which he learned to speak (and sing) fluent French. Returning stateside, he studied for a couple of degrees in vocal performance in Philadelphia, but soon enough realized it was no way to make a living. Fate would have it that he met a famous Spanish tenor who was giving a master class. The tenor told the class that he elected to pick and choose his engagements rather than make his life on the road. He spent the rest of the year selling real estate on the coast of Spain. Not slow to take the hint, Bob's opera career slowly but surely went by the wayside, even as his real estate career flourished. He now had plenty to eat, but was, at age 55, hungry! Soon it was off to Beijing with Claudia to cut a CD—"An American Tenor in China."

Our little company includes (among others) a Montessori teacher, a pastor, an environmental engineer, a Wal-Mart shipping manager (who in college had some serious training as a makeup artist), a fisheries expert, a retired video producer, two college students, a high school student, a middle school student, an insurance company clerk, another realtor, a mental health counselor, a construction worker, a coffee barista, and a soldier. Funny where you find opera singers these days.

Oh, so what did we sing? Bizet's *Carmen*. Wholesome family entertainment. Lots of sex and sexual innuendo, jealousy, lying, cheating, violence, intrigue, murder, cruelty toward animals, alcohol abuse, and ethnic stereotyping. Typical operatic fare, the same sort of stuff our kids should be learning when they study the Roman Empire. Lots of gyrating hips, though, unlike in the opera *Salomé*, we all got to keep our clothes on. Most prominent of all, risqué tobacco use—we should have attracted Philip Morris as a corporate sponsor. Among other roles in the chorus, Aliyah played a young woman working in a cigarette factory, who sings [in French of course, since the scene takes place in Seville (???)]:

Smoke rings make their lazy way,
Softly curling, softly curling,
Skyward they stray,
In a fragrant cloud unfurling.

Their perfume pervades the air,
Gently stealing, gently stealing,
Soothing our mind
To a mellow pleasant feeling.

Those tender words you lovers say
every day, fade away!
Your promises, too, like the smoke
in the blue, fade away.
Smoke rings rise and float away
In the blue of the sky.

See them curling and rising
And vanish at last in the blue of the sky.
See them rise,
To the skies!

I do so love the classics! (We found a great book on the history of *Carmen*, locating its context in 19th Century French cultural history). Before Opera Pacifica, the last time I had sung on a stage was in a "Fresh Air" camp for poor kids from New York City when I was 13. Now, I got to do my first-ever stage kiss, flirt with the cigarette girls, and sing the Toreador Song! And, by the end, my extremely meager French pronunciation likely approached Haitian (Aliyah's is much better, and with apologies to those from this studiously unstudied Caribbean island which staged the first and only successful national slave revolt in the history of the world—you do have that one marked in your homeschooling history books, right?)

"In Hoquiam, of all places," Aliyah and I kept repeating to each other, reinforcing each other's prejudices, having sung the opera twice in Olympia, our own booming metropolis of a state capital. Hoquiam is an old logging town that has been in serious decline for decades. Its population peaked in 1930, and now numbers under 11,000. Half the town seems boarded up, the other half seems about ready to fall down.

The performance was to be a fundraiser. A beautiful theater had been constructed in 1927, when the timber boom was in full swing. Spanish-style stucco walls, fine grillwork balconies, rococo columns, colorful light fixtures, painted, exposed-beam ceilings. It must have been a magnificent place in its time. But our fundraiser was to deal with the reality that the roof is caving in.

So who would come? Would you believe 700 people? If they were all from Hoquiam (about 75 percent were; the rest from a slightly larger town of 20,000 people next door), that would represent roughly 7 percent of the town's population—including children and shut-ins! Except the hall was filled with children, and the elderly, and the town council, and lumbermen and fisherfolk and car salesmen and bankers and supermarket checkout clerks. They cheered lustily throughout the performance, and they cheered afterwards, and we all joined them in the lobby to thank them for coming.

Bob and Claudia already have a sparkle in their eyes. This could be the perfect location for a regular opera summer festival, like they have in Spoleto, Italy, and Charleston, South Carolina (if you live on that other coast, in late May/early June this *is* the place to be! www.spoletousa.org) People would flock to the coast to fish and swim and hike and play golf, and spend the evening at the opera. The Hoquiam Chamber of Commerce would no longer be an oxymoron. We could be part of rescuing an entire town!

Next up? *The Marriage of Figaro.* The two of us have to brush up on our Italian.

Nice to be homeschooling!

Meera's Graduation

We are celebrating.

Meera (almost 13—my, how time flaps its wings!) is giving up the flute.

No, it's not what you think, and, no, I am not being sarcastic. Meera doesn't sound at all bad. In fact, she's absolutely terrific, and that was part of what led her to her decision.

The piano has always been Meera's first love, and remains so. She took up the flute after watching her sister rake in nickels, dimes, quarters, dollars, (and occasional $20's!) at street fairs and farmers' markets by playing her violin, enough to pay for a new instrument, a telescope-making workshop, a wolf-tracking expedition in Idaho, a folk harp and some lessons. The main attraction of the flute, initially, was that 1) it was portable; and 2) through my wife, we already had one. A better flute was eventually necessary, and materialized at just the proper moment on eBay.

It didn't take long for Meera to become quite adept at her instrument. A couple of listens to James Galway's renditions of "Oh Danny Boy", the Beatle's "In My Life", and Eric Clapton's "Tears in Heaven", the addition of several Broadway show tunes, the Shaker hymn "Simple Gifts", and a sprinkling of Bach and Handel, and she was ready for prime time. "For My New Puppy," the sign handsomely scrawled and attached to a shoebox, brought in the cash, sometimes at an alarming rate. To my way of thinking, we already had a perfectly acceptable canine, a large but docile half-Airedale/half-German Shepherd who thinks she is a miniature Cocker and wants to climb on our laps, but Meera desired a Westie—a BIG dog in a little body—more in keeping with her own personality.

In short order, the required $450 was amassed, and Duncan the Sugar Donut was now usurping my place on the couch. On occasion, Meera would still go down to the farmers' market with the same sign, only now with puppy in tow. The rate of accumulation doubled. This was somewhat puzzling, given that the little white fur ball had already made his appearance, but I think folks believed they were now contributing to Duncan's college education, and he seems, unlike our yellowish-brown carpet dweller, intelligent enough to likely benefit from it.

Meera soon enrolled in our local youth symphony, and learned all the little rituals and dress codes and conventions that come with playing formally with a group of people. She was pleased that the flutes didn't sit right out front, exposed to direct public scrutiny. She made friends quickly with her fellow flautists, commented once that the first trumpeter was cute, and seemed to be holding her own just fine, with very little practice to speak of.

That's exactly what made the enterprise begin to unravel. Meera is *good*, so good in fact that, with a little effort, she might have competed successfully for a place in the senior orchestra, occupied mostly by high school juniors and seniors. But she would lose the social benefits of playing with her chronological peers in the junior symphony. The flipside, however, is that the current music staples offered her little in the way of challenge and, as her piano repertoire is expanding rapidly, conspicuously less so as time goes on. In short, she was somewhat trapped by her giftedness.

Quakers have an aphorism that when things do not seemingly present themselves with an easy or obvious direction, we say the "way will open". And, sure enough, it did. Last summer, Meera went with a cousin of ours to an evening of modern jazz at a local cafe. (Olympia, as it turns out, has a relatively disproportionate share of fine musicians in all genres—jazz, rock, classical, folk, even opera!) At the end of the evening, as the venue was emptying out, Meera stepped up to the piano, and played from memory the classical version of a piece of Spanish music that the combo had turned into one of its own numbers. Instant sparks! She immediately befriended the 55-year-old saxophonist, stricken with childhood polio, but who had earlier in his career played with the jazz legend John Coltrane (with whom Meera was already familiar.) (There's more about Meera's "meeting up" with the adult world in "Meera's New Friends"; if you want to, skip ahead. Don't worry—I won't mind, and no one else will know.)

Now they spend literally hours on the phone together talking about jazz and life (and all those things that are easier *not* to talk about with your parents when you're 12.). She occasionally goes over to his house to listen to rehearsals (ironically, his wife is a flautist), and is soaking it all in. The saxophonist is undertaking to teach her jazz theory.

And Meera knows what she wants to do. Without at all abandoning the two hours she spends each day at the piano with her classical repertoire, she wants jazz vocal lessons. It is as if things have come full circle, or at least a turn of the spiral is completed. Six years ago, Meera taught herself to read by following along in the words as she learned to play Gershwin standards. Michael Feinstein and Ella Fitzgerald (with a little Laura Nyro thrown into the mix) were constant companions. Now, Diana Krall CDs are coming home from the library, and "Besame Mucho" is number one on our household's current hit parade. Who knows what's next?

In the meantime, we've invited Richard the flute teacher over for dinner and a celebration. We want to commemorate the event. We expect to do some picture-taking—of him, Meera, and Duncan of course—spend some time listening to their combined repertoire, and sharing some non-alcoholic toasts. Maybe we'll invite the jazz people over, too. There will be some presents—for both teacher and graduate—and perhaps I'll convince Aliyah to compose a flute duet for the occasion. ("Bad idea," says my wife, who is *always* right about these things, "should be for flute and piano.") Then the flute will be laid carefully and ceremonially in its case. Another learning adventure brought to successful fruition, and another one launched. Not a quitter, but a graduate. I can barely wait for the next episode!

P.S. Meera's flute will not be reappearing on eBay any time soon; I have my suspicions that we haven't heard the last of it yet.

Life is a Cabaret

What good is sitting alone
In your room?
Come hear the music play,
Life is a Cabaret, old chum,
Come to the Cabaret.

Put down the knitting,
The book and the broom,
Time for a holiday,
Life is a Cabaret, old chum,
Come to the Cabaret.

—from *Cabaret*,
Music by John Kander,
Lyrics by Fred Ebb

So here I am sitting alone in my room. That's what writers do, generally speaking. Whether any good will come of it shall really be yours to decide, not mine, so I'm off the hook at least in that regard.

Aliyah got herself a paid professional gig this summer, before going off to college, sniff, sniff. She was hired to play the violin in a theatrical version of *Cabaret*, being performed in our fair city. It was a rather risqué performance of a show that is fairly raunchy to begin with (the film version with Liza Minelli and Joel Gray was, shall we say, expurgated to play in… now I'm about to get myself in trouble…how about "places that appreciate good clean fun"?)

But no matter what is done with it, *Cabaret* will never pass as 'wholesome family entertainment'. Watching the local middle school bassoon teacher traipse around suggestively in revealing lingerie while singing lines chockfull of sexual innuendo would have been quite an eye-opener for many of the local kids, and the families were warned. At minimum, an "R" rating.

The pit orchestra for *Cabaret* didn't sit in the pit at all, but on the stage itself. Required uniform for Aliyah was a short, black, clingy, slightly revealing slip, with black boots and black fishnet stockings, black dangling earrings, black eye shadow, dark lipstick. This rather Goth get-up does not conform to her usual taste in clothing, which tends toward thrift-store neo-hippy. She seemed to be concerned about folks she knew catching a glimpse of her in *Cabaret* attire outside of the theatre, and so would throw her loose-fitting Mamas and Papas Indian blouse and skirt over the requisite Manson Family Wear. (Oh, wait, I've got that wrong! Manson Family Wear WAS thrift-store neo-hippy; I'm confusing them with Marilyn Manson! Delightful how aging enables us to be creatively anachronistic.)

Life is a Cabaret. Reminds us immediately that we consciously or unconsciously live our lives in metaphor. As an amateur storyteller, I have learned repeatedly that stories are by definition metaphorical, even when we don't notice it. That is, if we find nothing in the tale—characters, storyline, images, situations—with which we can find analogies in our own lives, it will fail to connect. Indeed, we sometimes characterize the richness of a story by the degree to which it acts as a metaphorical expression of our own inner or outer experience. The very essence of story is metaphor.

Learning, too. We work from the known to the unknown. We copy and adapt that which we see others do, finding analogues between their efforts and our own. We seek out role models, or they simply roll out right in front of us. We learn the same way every other mammal in the animal kingdom does. Instinct plays its part. For the rest, we watch and listen, try and err, hopefully not fatally, and grow in the process. We are like baby elephants, except that our symbolic abilities, our capacity for metaphor, allow us to learn from the experience of all those mothers and fathers who came before, or those whose banana leaves may have been pulled from trunks (and by their trunks) thousands of miles away.

'Educators' have another metaphor in mind. Dr. Frank Smith, in his superb must-read for homeschoolers *The Book of Learning and Forgetting* (New York, NY: Teachers College Press, 1998), notes how the metaphors used in educational circles these days betray modern education's origin in the Prussian military of the early 19th Century:

> We talk of the *deployment* of resources, the *recruitment* of teachers and students, *advancing* or *withdrawing* students, *promotion* to higher grades, *drills* for learners, *strategies* for teachers, *batteries* of tests, word *attack* skills, attainment *targets*, *reinforcement*, cohorts, *campaigns* for achievement in mathematics, and *wars* against illiteracy.

Without belaboring the obvious, it seems it has become almost impossible to talk, and hence to think, about the *business* of education (note the metaphor—who is "buying" and who is "selling", and what exactly is it that is being bought and sold?) without resorting to language strongly suggesting the infiltration of lockstep militaristic thinking. And it is easy to see how use of the underlying metaphors *education is a battlefield* and *teachers are enlisted men (and women) fighting for the minds of our youth* structures our thinking. Just imagine how different it would be—how different we would *make it be*—if we were to think in a different underlying metaphor, such as *education is a carnival or a county fair* or *school is a circus*.

I have to admit, though I didn't remember it at the time I first conceived of it, that this notion is not original with me. (From experience, I long ago came to the conclusion that, whatever my other redeeming qualities, I am just not *that* original, and if what I am contemplating is totally new, chances are it's wrong.) So for you lovers of classical education, how 'bout a low-brow serialized novel? Anyone remember Dickens' *Hard Times*? Don't be scared off: it is his shortest one—no *Bleak House* or *David Copperfield* here; you might actually find the time to read it. The book opens upon a school founder and overseer, the "eminently practical" Thomas Gradgrind, addressing his newest schoolmaster-trainee, one Mr. M'Choakumchild (Dickens lets you know very quickly where he stands, doesn't he?):

> "Now, what I want is, Facts. Teach these boys and girls nothing but Facts. Facts alone are wanted in life. Plant nothing else, and root out everything else. You can only form the minds of reasoning animals upon Facts: nothing else will ever be of any service to them. This is the principle on which I bring up my own children, and this is the principle on which I bring up these children. Stick to Facts, Sir!"

In the second chapter, we are treated to a demonstration of this method, coupled with an insight of how a commitment to *Fact*s would ensure the regulation of everyday life:

> "We hope to have, before long, a board of fact, composed of commissioners of fact, who will force the people to be a people of fact, and of nothing but fact. You must discard the word Fancy altogether. You must have nothing to do with it. You are not to have, in any object of use or ornament, what would be a contradiction in fact. You don't walk upon flowers in fact; you cannot be allowed to walk upon flowers in carpets. You don't find foreign birds and

butterflies come and perch upon your crockery; you cannot be permitted to paint foreign birds and butterflies upon your crockery. You never meet with quadrupeds going up and down walls; you must not have quadrupeds represented upon walls."

And so on and so forth. The entire novel is built around the failure of this educational approach (coupled with the unscrupulousness of politicians and the pompous duplicity of the industrialists of Coketown—a city which is "a triumph of fact" as they grind the life out of their workers), and the ruin it brings down about the Gradgrind family and everyone else within their compass.

Dickens is quick to present his educational foil, and, wouldn't you know it, it is a traveling circus carnival—"Sleary's Horse-Riding"—that produces our heroine, Sissy Jupe (who is quickly deemed 'uneducable' once consigned to Gradgrind's keeping*).* Sleary's Horse-Riding is an extended family of acrobats, twirlers, riders, and animal trainers, who entertain through "pleasing but always strictly moral wonders" (no *Cabaret* here), and who care for each other in the rough-and-tumble of perpetual life on the road:

> They were all assumed to be mighty rakish and knowing, they were not very tidy in their private dresses, they were not at all orderly in their domestic arrangements, and the combined literature of the whole company would have produced but a poor letter on any subject. Yet there was a remarkable gentleness and childishness about these people, a special inaptitude for any kind of sharp practice, and an untiring readiness to help and pity one another, deserving often of as much respect, and always of as much generous construction, as the every-day virtues of any class of people in the world.

What if, implies Dickens, what if, demands the homeschooling author, sitting alone in his room, we were to make it our calling—our *business* (there goes that discomforting metaphor again)—to interject a heady dose of "Sleary's Horse-Riding" into that all-too-solemn world of grade levels, credential-chasing, and future college admissions?

Well, I've "put down the knitting"—actually never learned how. (Got to add that to the long list of my deficiencies.) If my room is any indication, I "put down the broom" (and the vacuum cleaner) a long time ago, (or maybe I never picked them up.) No, you CAN'T have my books! But I'll give you the rest (ritard, forcefully, with feeling). Hit it!:

Start by admitting,
From cradle to tomb
Isn't that long a stay.
Life is a Cabaret, old chum,
Only a Cabaret, old chum,

And I love a Cabaret.

Meera's New Friends

It was like someone threw a switch. At ages 10 and 11, all of Meera's interests were centered around her age-bound peers. Bicycling around the neighborhood, trips to the mall, even "study" sessions were just the coolest thing. (Sic! these last surely weren't *my* idea of a good time, and I have no idea what she was studying with her school-imprisoned buddies when they were out on work-release.) For a while, she and her best friend tried to compare menus before deciding where dinner was to be had (an effort that was soon quashed by the cooks who found themselves unable to plan.) I am sure (based on my own childhood experience) that they probably spent a good part of the time listening to music of which they thought their parents disapproved, discussing the evils of the world, and, especially, the fact that most of the adults they know are either unjust or, at the very least, hypocrites. (We *are*, of course, as all 11-year-olds are only too well aware.)

And then, as if part of some predetermined plan, virtually exactly on her 12th birthday, new lights went on. A middle-aged cousin, Susan, invited Meera to a meeting of an ongoing adult Muslim-Jewish "compassionate listening" dialogue group. Being neither an adult, nor Muslim, nor Jewish did not prove to be a hindrance to participation, and soon stacks of books from the library on world religions made it to her room (this came as quite a shock, as Meera is a reluctant, even if adept, reader.) Soon, she befriended a childless middle-aged library computer specialist and her husband, both members of our Quaker Meeting, who had recently returned from peace missions to Israel and Palestine. Now she began attending slideshows and presentations in area churches, and the newspaper (and the much-ignored world map on the wall) took on new meaning.

Donna and her husband Mark are also avid supporters of the local animal shelter, and Meera began to tag along on regular volunteer visits. And they began to share an ongoing interest in photography. Meera attended an uncle's wedding in New Orleans, and immediately struck up a long-distance relationship with the photographer, a friend of said uncle, who lives in Boston, and she took to calling him up and picking his brain about the photography business.

Meanwhile, Cousin Susan reappeared, and took Meera out for an evening of modern jazz. At the end of the concert, as folks filed out, having just heard a jazz arrangement of a tango by the Spanish composer Isaac

Meera with Bert Wilson, November, 2003.

Albeniz, Meera strode up to the piano and floored them with the classical version, note perfect from memory. And so began a new relationship, this time with the saxophonist. Bert, now in his 60s, is an extraordinarily gifted player (once played with John Coltrane) and arranger (see www.bertwilson. com). He was also stricken with childhood polio and is confined to a wheelchair. Bert and Meera spend hours on the phone together, discussing jazz theory, Bert's bout with polio, or just life in general. On occasion, when she can't make it over to Bert's house to watch the rehearsals, Meera will dial in while they are going on, and keeps the phone receiver next to her pillow as she falls asleep (that's why we can "never" find the phone!)

As a result of her relationship with Bert, Meera has decided to supplement her classical piano studies with jazz vocal lessons. She also developed an intense interest in disease processes, and read several books on the polio epidemic of the 1950s. One of them, it turns out, was written by a woman who lives approximately 90 miles from our home, and Meera started up a written correspondence.

Donna noticed that through this entire period, Meera had developed a strong interest in individuals' personal histories. When two members of our Meeting announced that they were moving away, Donna suggested Meera write their life stories for the Meeting newsletter. Meera worked up a list of questions, set up interview time, and began her career as Meeting biographer. The Meeting also provided Meera with her first foray into marriage counseling. A couple within the Meeting, including a woman who had once been a babysitter for Meera a decade earlier, had split up, and Meera spent hours on the phone, virtually every evening for a month with each of them, and was in no little measure responsible for a trial reconciliation. Alas, it was not to be. But, in short, within a span of six months, Meera went from having absolutely no visible interest in the adult world, to an interest in virtually nothing else.

So what has Meera been *learning* lately? Well, there's politics, and history, and geography, and comparative religion, and photography, and science, and music, and writing, and "social skills", and…. Yes, we could compartmentalize it if we wanted to, but to do so would be to miss the point entirely. Life is not pigeonholed into subject matter, but the subject matter itself only takes on meaning in the context of enduring human and social relationships. And, in the case of Meera, newly emerging ones.

This is the lesson all early teens require. Instead of hothousing the kids, we need to provide the scaffolding so that they can get out into the world, try on futures for themselves like so many hats, find mentors, understand the workings of their community and the places of individuals within it, and, above all, find ways to contribute.

And they are hungry for it. They have already figured out that we (as parents) are not going to be around forever, or in the shorter term, they may come to the limits of our hospitality. They will need to learn to fly, but at some point we become the very worst persons to provide pilot training.

The trick is to find ways for them to connect. Homeschooling a young teen should *never* be business as usual. She is confronting a new body, a new sense of self, new intellectual and emotional capacities, new intimations of a future into which we ourselves, ultimately, are refused entry. If you find yourselves with your young teen doing "the same old, same old", you can be pretty sure you are doing the wrong thing. Instead of treating your young ones as overgrown children, increasingly large and difficult to control (in school, they would be the new subjects of metal detectors), think of them as intrepid travelers heading out on their maiden voyage, and you are providing them with a directory of interesting places and an address book and letters of introduction to people who might be able to help them out along the way.

Having trouble finding a bridge into the mentoring/apprenticeship/adult-world participation thing for your son and daughter? I know (from having spoken to enough homeschooling parents) that despite all the suggestions I make (you can find a long list of them in *Homeschooling and the Voyage of Self-Discovery*), some kids are just not ready to make the leap easily, and, given the larger societal context in which young teens find themselves these days, that is not surprising. But I do have a suggestion: community interviewing. Have your kids go out and really meet the people that make up their world, and have them write it up. If your homeschool group has a significant number of younger teens, they can do it as a group, and combine the stories into a community notebook, complete with photographs (find someone to teach photography, too.) Interview the mayor, the local pastor, the dentist, the beautician, your next-door neighbor—have the kids find out what makes each of them tick.

To do this right, help your child draw up a list of questions in advance. You can also teach interviewing skills. In one of my books—*The Healing Heart~Communities: Storytelling to Build Strong and Healthy Communities* (New Society, 2003)—the storyteller Doug Lipman offers a series of games for teaching interviewing techniques, especially those that can elicit stories from those being interviewed. Practice can transform the process of going out to meet the world from a perilous journey to an exciting adventure.

That's precisely what it is supposed to be. And, yes, they can still use their bikes to get there (until they start asking for the family car....)

* * * * *

I came home from a speaking tour in the Midwest to be informed that Meera was planning to perform a benefit concert. This one caught my wife and me entirely by surprise. She had made it clear to us in no uncertain terms that, despite her extraordinary gift, she hates playing the piano in public. She had played her debut recital, and, as far as she was concerned, it was also her swansong. We had no sense that she was in any way likely to end up as a Glenn Gould, the reclusive, hypochondriac piano virtuoso who, before his death, hadn't played in public for almost 40 years. We told her that this was totally fine with us (which I think may have annoyed her just a little bit.) Actually, it was. After all, we get a private concert every night, so we are hardly in a position to complain.

So how did this all come about? This is what I was told, though I have heard there are other versions. Seems that Meera was sitting on Donna's porch one afternoon. Our town—Olympia, Washington—is now a pretty touchy place when it comes to Israeli-Palestinian issues. We are the hometown of Rachel Corrie, a former student at the local Evergreen State College, who was killed when she attempted to block an Israeli bulldozer from razing a Palestinian doctor's home in Gaza. The Jewish community often feels under siege, despite the fact that they play absolutely no role in the actions of the Israeli military, regardless of how one might feel about them, and most, in this predominantly liberal community, likely do not support the more extreme actions of the Israeli government.

So Donna and Mark were talking about the need to create a safe venue for dialogue for the whole community. Through previous travels, Donna had met members of a group called the "Israeli-Palestinian Families of the Bereaved Forum for Peace" (www.theparentscircle.com). These are families who have lost family members—fathers and mothers, brothers and sisters, sons and daughters—and have now banded together across the divide to support each other, create opportunities for dialogue between them, and to help to create an atmosphere of peaceful dialogue around the world. The problem was that there were no funds to bring representatives—one Israeli, one Palestinian—to Olympia.

"I know how to get money," said Meera.

Off they went. Ellen and I suggested that she do a series of house concerts, perhaps a little less stressful, but Meera was adamant.

"If I'm going to do this, I'm only going to do this once, and I want a *big* audience because, after all, *they need the money.*" She had only two conditions: her piano teacher wasn't invited, and she didn't want any comments on her playing.

Meera with Ghazi and Rami, November 2003.

Donna rented the largest church hall with a good piano she could find. Meera came out and played a brilliant recital (whoops, sorry for the adjective! I'm not supposed to say that, and for the most part I was pretty good about keeping my big mouth shut, which can be quite a chore!) of Bach, Beethoven, Schubert, Chopin, Albeniz, Schubert, Granados, Rachmaninoff, and Khachaturian. We had a sign-up sheet for those who wished to purchase a CD of the concert, and we ended up selling more than a hundred of them. We held a big, post-concert dinner in one of Meera's favorite restaurants. After all was said and done, Meera had raised more than $1,800.

Rami Elhanan and Ghazi Brigieth came to town. Rami's 14-year-old daughter was killed in a Jerusalem suicide bombing (and, poignantly, Meera somewhat resembles her.) Ghazi lost two brothers, the younger, age 14, shot on the way home from school. More than 1,500 people attended a series of meetings and facilitated dialogues in churches, the synagogue, the Friends Meetinghouse. When a piano was available, Meera would introduce them with a sad Chopin waltz in a minor key.

Following the meetings in Olympia, Meera spent most of three days accompanying them to other areas in Washington State. Now she has two new families, 8,000 miles away!

Meera composed an article about her experiences, which was quickly accepted for publication in a West Coast Quaker journal. She wrote:

> The first time I had the privilege of listening to Rami and Ghazi speak in Olympia, it was a very inspiring and motivating experience. The next time it was very upsetting; it just became more saddening to hear all of their tragedies for the second time. The last time I heard them, it almost became frustrating. It seemed so incredible that at one time they had so much anger or hate inside. Yet they were able to take all of that anger, and turn it around not into retaliation or revenge, but into more love and compassion for the Israelis, Palestinians, and people everywhere.
>
> It is very sad to know that I have only heard two people in this kind of situation speak, only three days out of my whole life, and after these three days it seemed to be one of the most overwhelming experiences ever. So I can't even begin to imagine what it would be like to live with the pain of losing you daughter or brother, and have to live with that pain every day of your life, and yet still have the strength to promote, and encourage peace and justice in the amazing way these two people do.

* * * * *

Meera fired the piano teacher shortly after the concert, or perhaps it is more politic to say they fired each other. I think he was miffed by the whole recital thing happening without him. He wanted her to play in piano competitions, and Meera was quite firm that wasn't going to happen. Meera is absolutely appalled by the idea that music can be competitive (and as an advanced gymnast, she knows what competition is about.) What fun is it to have a star pupil if no one else gets to hear her? Meera had clear ideas about the music she wished to study—always two or three steps ahead of where her technical prowess was currently, allowing her to pull herself up with huge amounts of driven energy. He liked to go one step at a time. He dreamed of a concert pianist; she dreamed of feeding her own ear, and her sense of herself and the world of musical possibilities. They had a less-than-happy parting of the ways.

We went hunting for teachers. The chairs of the piano faculties at two local universities seemed to fit the bill, though we could see Meera was uneasy. And then one said something that immediately struck a chord: she really doesn't want a teacher, she wants a coach! We thought about her relationship with her gymnastics coach, and how they work together, and it just rang true.

The coach became… (big breath)… me! I don't play a note. But it's not as crazy as it seems. Dave, Meera's male gymnastics coach, obviously never did women's gymnastics either (actually, he never did *any* gymnastics, and while he was quite an athlete in his day, never had any education or training in coaching gymnastics or in coaching, period. This year, all six of his eligible advanced gymnasts qualified for the national championships.) I don't play the piano, and I play the violin, well, indifferently would be a compliment, but I do sing opera, played south Indian music for a long time, have a very well-developed musical ear, and know a lot about what's in the basic repertoire. I have heard more than a few of the world's great pianists, and I have a good sense what it's supposed to sound like, even if I have no real idea of how one goes about producing it. Like the gymnastics coach, I developed almost all of these interests long after my formal schooling came to an end. I have three advantages over virtually any music teacher I've ever met: I have no particular expectations; I know my student really, really well; and, more often than not (though I'm still struggling), I know how to get out of the way! And I have a fourth very real advantage over many: I am still in an active process of learning music, and how to coach, and so we are learning together. Meera is as often my teacher as I am hers.

So what do we do? Well, we choose music together. She's a young teenager, and likes to wear her heart on her sleeve, with big gestures. Chopin and Rachmaninoff. She has a very special way with Spanish music, which is reinforced by her often hearing it on the gym floor. She's added the music of the great Cuban composer Ernesto Lecuona, rarely played other than his *Malagueña*, to her repertoire. She thought she didn't like French music, until I introduced to the gentleness and nuanced beauty of Debussy. She dreams of Mussorgsky's *Pictures at an Exhibition*—okay, I say, but we agree to spend not less than 18 months learning it; there's no rush to go anywhere. I have finally convinced her to explore the more rigorous pianist harmonies of Schumann and Brahms; she already knows she can play some of the big Beethoven sonatas, so we are going to leave him alone for awhile. A trip to the music store is a real family outing, and fun! but one for which I actually have to study.

Then what happens? Well, we meet, or more accurately, I listen, with full, uninterrupted attention, one hour a week. By the time I get to listen, she has already taught herself the notes, and is playing up close to full speed. She doesn't need me for that, and I couldn't help her in any case. I coach "music", not "notes". She reads piano music much, much better than I do (she can sightread most anything), and she doesn't need me to train her fingers! In fact, it is virtually a rule we have together that I don't correct any note mistakes she makes, unless I am convinced she has read the notes incorrectly. Otherwise, she knows full well when she has played something in error, and chances are I'll never hear the same mistake again. So if it isn't up to speed yet, or the notes aren't yet mastered, we put the piece of music away for a future week, or make an agreement that she'll be ready with a portion of it (she likes to start at the beginning, I like to start in the middle, and sometimes we compromise; the rest of the time she wins.) So I sit, and we work on dynamics, expression, timbre (I can't produce it, but I can often give her the sense by singing it). I provide alternative suggestions of tempi, which she can accept or reject as she chooses. Sometimes I'll bring contrasting recordings home from the library, so she can compare and make more informed choices. We think together. Mostly, I just sit there, and pinch myself. I often tell her to breathe.

The rest? She spends about 75 minutes at the piano "practicing" every day. Some days more, some days less. Given the level of music she is playing at this point, most teachers would expect 3 to 4 hours. Tough! The thing is, Meera breathes music. She actually spends on average much more than her practice time at the piano. Sometimes it will be playing jazz. Sometimes just browsing music books. Sometimes there is a new obsession in a piece she's learning.

I would be the first one to admit that Meera is blessed with a very unusual, and rare, natural gift. Certainly, I know that I could practice the piano eight hours a day for the rest of my natural life (and perhaps an unnatural one as well!) and not get to her level of proficiency. The same would hold true for Aliyah her sister, who, although also a very talented musician, has very different gifts.

But it would be easy to lose the real lesson in this atypicality, for in the very intensity of Meera's gift, one finds crystallized that which can—which *must*—propel children—*all children*—on their expeditions of discovery.

If we look deeply, I believe it is possible to find the engines within that enable children to move forward in their learning enterprises. Courage, to encounter the new and strange, and make them freshly a part of one's expanding sense of self-in-the-world. Heart, and the internalized realization that one learns through trial and error, and that without error, there is no learning that is long-lasting. To err is human, and, if I may be so bold, it also contains within it the seed of the divine. A ferocious stick-to-it-iveness, a capacity for going beyond the expectations of others, or for putting those expectations aside in the knowledge quest. Commitment, not to perfection, but to growth, and an expanding acknowledgment that growth takes time.

If I were a wagering man (I'm not—Quakers don't wager, or at least some of us think we're not supposed to), I'd bet that if you examine those successful knowledge quests you've undertaken in your own life, you will find these same characteristics. And, I'd further venture that, for many of us, much of what we've had to overcome to be successful in these voyages are attitudes toward learning, and toward ourselves, that we've internalized as a result of our "educations", so that we can rediscover courage, heart, intensity, and commitment. I've spent much of the past 35 years in the process of this rediscovery, and, indeed, that is much of what this book is all about.

* * * * *

Adrien Niyangabo came to town. It was one of those transformative experiences that sometimes come forth unasked, and we are still experiencing the results. He was invited to Olympia to give a talk to a small group of interested folks, mostly from local churches, and organized by a couple new to our Friends Meeting who have been taking in some of the "lost boys" of the Sudan. My kids were the only young people in attendance (it was a "school" night.)

Adrien comes from Bujumbara, the capital of Burundi in central Africa. He was in some sense already marked for a very special role in life by the fact that his mother was a Tutsi, and his father a Hutu, in a country when more than a million people have been killed and almost another million made homeless by Hutus and Tutsis killing each other and burning each others' villages. On October 23rd, 1993, as a university student, he was fleeing Tutsi soldiers, only to be marked for death by Hutus seeking revenge for the assassination of the Hutu President of Burundi, and saved at the very last moment by a gunman confused about his identity.

In 2000, with the help of Quakers from abroad, Adrien co-founded the Healing and Rebuilding Our Communities program of the African Great Lakes Initiative. The program goes into the camps of internally displaced persons and facilitates face-to-face trauma healing workshops between members of both groups, who will eventually be returning to what is left of their homes in the same communities. Victims directly confront killers, only to find out that, in many instances, the killers are victims themselves. Some of the results have been extraordinary. In one case, a group of Tutsi widows, determined to prepare the way for their children and grandchildren, have gone to regional prisons to meet with imprisoned Hutu officials to express their forgiveness. Youth who have never spoken to each other and have lived most of their lives in the camps (and who are the likely targets of recruiting for new ethnic violence) are brought together to grieve, learn new skills, and effect the beginnings of reconciliation.

Although still a young man, with three young children of his own, Adrien was like an Old Testament prophet. In telling his story, very quietly and in an almost matter-of-fact manner, he had the few of us in attendance close to tears. Peace was possible, even in the midst of genocide, even when governments were among the guilty, even when the international community had deserted them. The Peaceable Kingdom was at hand, the lion could lie down with the lamb, especially when it was actually impossible to ascertain which was lamb and which lion.

The Friends Meeting decided to launch a new initiative to provide micro-economic loans and small grants to individuals and families leaving the camps for displaced persons to return home. Even $30 could pay for a pair of goats, or a few agricultural implements, or some seed for the first planting. Meera decided to kick off the campaign with a benefit concert. She has spent much of the past several months learning about Africa, the history of colonialism, and the work of Alternatives to Violence Projects around the world. As word of her efforts spread, she was invited to fly across the country to repeat her recital at First Old Reformed Church in Philadelphia, with Adrien speaking at the intermission.

Now Meera's network of new friends has expanded internationally, to Israel-Palestine, to central Africa, and to southern India, where Aliyah and I went this past winter to help with tsunami relief efforts (you can read our daily blog at shantinik.blogspot.com). Aliyah is returning this summer to continue the work by helping to build houses with flood and tsunami victims.

Meera with Adrien Niyangabo (and lion and lamb) at Philadelphia benefit concert for the African Great Lakes Initiative, April 2005.

(Pictures can be found at www.lafti.net). Our daughters have become risk-takers and bridge-builders, our family world citizens.

We have become SERVAS hosts. SERVAS is an international organization with 14,000 families and individuals in more than 130 countries. We offer hospitality to travelers from every nation, race, culture, and religion, in the pursuit of peace and global understanding, one family at a time. It allows us to become tourists in our own home.

Meera now wants to go to Burundi.

(P.S. She still bikes around the neighborhood.)

* * * * *

For more information about SERVAS International, check out their website at www.servas.org. Note: you (or your children) can become SERVAS travelers when abroad without becoming SERVAS hosts, and when you get to experience hospitality around the world, your view of the globe is likely to be radically transformed. This could be one of the best things you could ever do for your family. (And don't worry about an unkempt house—the idea is that other people get to experience you as you are!)

More information about the African Great Lakes Initiative can be found at www.aglionline.org .

Finally, copies of the CD from Meera's benefit recital are available through my website: www.skylarksings.com Makes a great gift for that budding pianist, or for anyone who just likes good music played with passion.

My Special Skill

In November 2001, I broke my elbow. You see, the phone rang in the kitchen, and, heeding its demands, I executed an exquisite balletic leap over the dog gate (we confine the dogs to the "Doggie Zone", which consists of the kitchen and the family room.) It was a wonderful leap, graceful and perfect in every way, but just at the precise moment that my leap reached its apex, the dog gate leapt too! SPLAT! Down I went in a heap. Pain! But actually more shock than pain. Still lying there, I checked for blood, as did Duncan (Meera's Westie), who assumed I'd belly-flopped to the floor in order to play with him, and he licked my nose. (Now it's becoming like one of those nighttime cop shows when the dog discovers the body.) Gracie—half-Airedale/half-German Shepherd—remained in her usual position, imitating, and camouflaged by, the carpet. (You've all seen her in the Westminster Kennel Club finals, representing the Resting Group.) No red stuff. Feet and legs work. Head okay. Left elbow broken.

I already knew it, so I picked myself up, and for the next 20 minutes wrestled with my violin. I figured (wrongly as it turned out) that it might be my last chance for a long time. No pain, and the violin (which should not be held responsible) sounded on the nether side of indifferent, as usual.

(I *am* an optimist, or so I am trying to convince myself, and there's always hope...) Then, my wife Ellen having returned, I helped carry the broken gas range around from the back of the house to the front, and loaded it on a truck to take to the town dump. Cooked dinner, and then drove the family downtown to a concert given by some of our friends. By nine o'clock, my face had turned pasty. But, it being Saturday night, there was no way I was going to the emergency room—it would have to wait till morning.

My elbow healed just fine, thank you, but I spent more than a year fighting with the emergency physicians and my health insurance company over a bill that had already been paid. Ah, this is America! I have started billing them both for my time in dealing with this matter—$50 an "encounter"— you should see the letters I get back! I have used all my writing skills to cajole, humor, excoriate, and threaten, and my entire panoply of professional negotiating skills, all for naught. I'd probably get an "A" in oral and written communications (I didn't let them see my penpersonship), and fat lot of good it has done me!

But back to my elbow. While I was lying on the floor, the very first thing that went through my mind was, I kid you not, "Will I still have my *special* skill?" You see, I do have this skill thing, and it *is* really special, maybe the most important thing I ever learned in school. I have entertained thousands of people with it over the course of my lifetime. Kids at homeschooling

conferences love it—they ask for it again and again, and enjoy hearing the story that goes with it.

My name begins with "A", and there were no "Aarons", "Adamses", "Adlers", or "Aardvarks" in my public school classes, and so for seven years of my life, 180-plus days a year, I was condemned to Row 1, Seat 1, right side, front, away from the window. That's more than 1,260 days, at least five hours a day, five days a week, looking left. For any permanent deformations I may have, I have an excuse!

Row 1, Seat 1 was usually out of the teacher's direct line of sight. Good thing, too, 'cause I fidgeted. I mean *really* fidgeted. I swung my legs left, and then right, and crossed them and uncrossed them, and rubbed my right leg with the sole of my left shoe, and my left leg with the heel of my right shoe, and tried to twist both legs simultaneously around the chair legs. (I once fell over in the attempt, and ended up with a bloody lip.) I tore off little pieces of paper, and attempted to shape them (unsuccessfully, I might add) into little birds, rats, turtles, cockroaches. I scribbled on the underside of the desk, and in the desk "pocket". I bit my nails and played with the "clippings", hence firmly establishing a habit that has stayed with me for a lifetime (I haven't used a set of nail clippers in 40 years).

I counted the number of people who went to the bathroom down the hall, (even timed them!), watched the shadows creep into the room as the

sky darkened in winter, and tried without success to teach myself to roll my tongue. Ah, I'd hit on one of those sad genetic truths, and try as I might, I would remain an underachiever.

I was (really!) a very good student, but I was bored. So bored. Really bored. Really, really bored! Really, really, REALLY B-O-R-E-D BORED!!! Bored Big-Time! And sometimes, as we all know, boredom can be the true mother of invention (as the late Frank Zappa used to remind us, "And in that magic go-kart, I bite your neck…" www.angelfire.com/hi/zuccaro/duke. html).

It happened when I was 11, I think. Having fidgeted enough with my fingers and toes that special day, I stuck both arms straight out, palms facing away from each other. Then I placed the right arm over the left one, and firmly interlaced my fingers. Then I rotated my hands down and under and out again, fingers still firmly interlaced. I placed the right elbow over the left elbow. And by jutting the right elbow out, I made a little square hole. And, for some reason, I left my arms in this position and stuck my head through the hole, arms sliding down the side of my face, past my ears, until my hands, still interlocked, sat on the back of my neck. As a final *coup de grace,* I snapped the left elbow up past the right one.

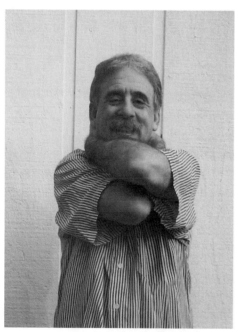

There you have it—my special skill. The culmination of seven years of public education. Now I know the school doesn't like to take responsibility, but I can say that, without any question, they are certainly at least as responsible for my special skill as they are for my ability to read or multiply (they wouldn't dare chose to take responsibility for my handwriting), or for my ability (or lack thereof) in dealing successfully with the insurance company. So I feel a need to give credit where credit is due. Kids began to gather round in the schoolyard, and I began to teach!

If you invite me to speak to your homeschool group, I'll try to teach it to all of you as best I can. To your kids, too. I'm soon hoping to cash in on an instructional video (write me!), and maybe, just maybe, Pay-Per-View! It can be our special sign, and take the place of a secret homeschool handshake. From experience, though, I have discovered that only about one in five people can manage anything close to it, about the same percentage of kids that seem to be passing some of the new high-stakes tests, or adults who, having gotten past the insult, actually stick with the Richard Simmons workout video they received for Christmas. We'll separate out the goats from the sheep!

But we'll have to try to keep it quiet, or, next thing we know, it might end up as one of the state's mandated learning objectives! So be careful to whom you give this essay—we wouldn't want it falling into the *wrong* hands.

Saint Riley Slocumb and the Maw of Hell

I wrote this for my kids. I'm always seeking ways to share with them the vagaries of the adult world, and the people that inhabit it. Many times, of course, they acquire this information through reading works of fiction. Sometimes, however, it is useful to allow a little reality to occupy the stage.

* * * * *

Transporting me on a recent trip to Dallas to deliver a series of homeschooling talks, United Airlines lost a box of my books. Seems that when I changed planes in Denver, one of the boxes accompanied me to Texas. The other had other plans, or at least there were other plans in store for it.

Disappointing, but far from the worst thing in the world. I had the notes for my talks with me in my carry-on, and even my clothes. Several boxes of books had arrived before me, and one was waiting at baggage claim. The plane hadn't crashed, or been rerouted by tornados; in fact, it wasn't even late.

Deep breath. "Don't sweat too hard about that which you have no control," I muttered to myself, as I made a firm decision to take it in stride. And I strode over to the United baggage claim office.

And there he was. Riley Slocumb. I discovered his name from the security badge hanging from his waist. Uniformed, but certainly not in any way that might command respect. Tie an inch too narrow, in keeping with a body too thin, not from diet or exercise, but from some kind of existential insult. Age indeterminate—I guessed 55—long, brown-gray hair slicked back high on the center of the scalp, bald spots pushing back from his temples on either side. We shared look-alike moustaches. Eyes not exactly dull, and not exactly bloodshot, not physically tired. Definitely world-weary.

"Rough day," I began, then realizing this was a very odd way to introduce myself.

He looked up from the standing desk.

"They lost one of my boxes," I sighed.

And then, first dimly, and then somewhat excitedly, I realized that from his point of view, there wasn't anything appropriate for him to do or say, other than deal with the mountain of paperwork.

You see, Riley can't put on a happy face and provide service with a smile. People, none of whom ever come to see him by choice, and all of whom would prefer not to even know he existed, might think he was mocking them. Commiseration is not what they desire, not from the appointed representative of the very company that had just shipped their new titanium-headed golf clubs to Bulgaria. They want action, they want answers, they want their bags and boxes and fishing poles and skis and children's car seats, and they want them *now*—and these are just the things he is virtually certain not to be able to provide.

Even before he could summon up a response to my question, and fully explain the paperwork, a violently energetic woman stormed into the office. Her gestures were writ large, and while I might have written that her painfully red hair was standing straight up, it would then have required a further note that the hair didn't know which way up was and so had, independently, decided to cover all the bases.

"She took my bag," the tsunami half-shouted.

"Who?" inquired Riley, careful not to offend, but also careful not to expend the daily allotment of concern. It was only 2 p.m., and it was going to be a long afternoon.

The story poured out. Two women had virtually identical black, rolling carry-on bags standing next to each other at the baggage claim ramp. The first woman, after grabbing her checked luggage, walked off with the wrong carry-on as well. She might be well on her way to the Presidential compound in Crawford by now, for all we knew. I looked down at my black, rolling carry-on bag, smug in spying the pink-and-white lace ribbon I had tied to it still affixed to the handle. "Good planning," I congratulated myself, using my mind to pat myself on the back. But I was caught up short by the disappointing realization that my good planning hadn't absented me from Riley Slocumb's acquaintance.

"I'm sorry, ma'am," said Riley, calibrating his comments carefully, "But we are not responsible for carry-on baggage."

"But, but..." sputtered the walking volcano, shaking from hair's end to feet, "all my travel information, my wallet, my cell phone, my hotel reservation, my address book, my...*everything is in that bag!*" I remembered my mother having taught me to never put the important stuff in checked baggage—always carry it with you on the plane. I shivered.

Riley paged his supervisor, and the supervisor and Mount St. Helen's went out into the baggage claim hall, where there was now an *unaccompanied* black bag. Yikes! I had visions they might have to call in the dog sniffers, or the bomb squad, or even evacuate the airport...and I hadn't filled in my paperwork yet. I picked up the pen. They simply took the questionable bag back to the supervisor's office, and spilled out the contents on his desk.

In Riley's office, air molecules were now slowing down, and new air filled the vacuum where the supervisor and Vesuvius had been. But before I could blurt out my next question, Riley now standing at his post writing, a short, middle-aged, mousy-blonde woman, her face covered in shame, sheepishly entered the room.

"I...I left my coat on the plane," she mumbled apologetically, looking humiliated, as if she had just told her mom she had lost her lunch money. "Can I go back and get it?"

"I'm sorry," replied Riley curtly, being careful not to look up, and punching numbers into an unseen machine below the countertop. "People aren't allowed into the restricted area without a ticket or boarding pass."

"Well," she pleaded, looking like she was about to burst into tears, "Can you check with the plane, please?"

"Flight number?"

"1252."

Riley picked up the blue phone. I think he had three phones—black, blue, and off-white—used for various parts of the airport.

"This is Charley-B. A women left a..." He looked up momentarily.

"Light red, cloth."

"A light red, cloth overcoat on flight..."

"1252."

"1252."

"Can you get back to me if you find it?" The tone of the question, intended to be overheard, sounded as if he wasn't very hopeful.

And now I realize that Riley's past two encounters, while not particularly unique, are somewhat unusual for him. For about 98 percent of the encounters he has, the customer is right. Right, not as in "The customer is *always* right," but really right, as in the airline has screwed up and the passengers' anger is justified. He can't smirk behind his back at customers who are being unreasonable, like the hotel concierge who makes fun of the guest who complains that the chocolates on the pillow are not of her favorite Belgian semi-sweet variety. No, people just want the belongings they had possessed only a few hours earlier. We feel, in some fundamental way, violated, and that, in having misplaced our luggage, they have taken away a piece of our identity. Now if they'd only allow us onto the tarmac....

"Are you here as a result of your karma, or are you being punished, or did you get this job as a promotion?" I ask, handing him the paperwork.

The shadow which has been inhabiting Riley's face lifts ever-so briefly as he glances at the papers. There has been real human contact, and, perhaps, someone else has glimpsed, if but momentarily, his daily predicament.

"Got any kids?" I smile.

"All grown."

"Dog?"

He smiles. We share an interest in preventing cruelty toward animals. He checks the computer. My box, he says, was checked onto the plane in Denver, which means it definitely made it to the Dallas airport.

"Can we inquire back at the place where they unloaded?" I ask, of course not knowing the first thing about how airport baggage handling works.

He picks up the blue phone. "This is Charlie-B. There's a box that should have come off Flight 748 that hasn't made it to baggage claim."

He has reached another operative on a blue phone, I assume. The baggage handlers have gone off to lunch.

'Do you drink?"

He grins. He is now into the spirit of our meeting for worship. "Gave it up years ago."

"Good thing," I reply.

I ended up waiting another 35 minutes by the baggage claim office. No box turns up. The frenzied and fuming, irate and irritated, miffed and peeved file their way toward Riley Slocumb. He hands out and assists in the completion of paperwork, being wary of offering anything that could remotely be construed as a promise, or arouse even the slightest wisp of expectation.

"If we find your luggage," he says to one and all with little in the way of feeling in his voice, "we will do our best to deliver it to you within 24 hours, so be sure to leave a phone number along with your address. And," he continues without the slightest hint of enthusiasm as he points to an 800-

number on the carbon-copy of the form, "you can call this number for any updates."

This was, of course, just a way to make sure folks would move along and out of his very circumscribed sphere of influence. I began to fantasize about how my box of homeschooling books made their way to Portugal, and was discovered by a baggage handler who took the books home to his family. Next thing I knew, three years later, I received an unsolicited invitation to address the newly formed Lisbon Home Education Association.

I now understand that I must get out of here. I am being sucked into this maw of hell, and if I stay much longer, I may not be able to leave. There should be a sign above the door to the baggage claim office, in the manner of Dante's Inferno, "Abandon all hope, all ye who enter here." I will leave Riley to confront his demons, not with flaming sword, but with a strangely courageous, saintly equanimity. A holy diffidence. Perhaps he has been specially selected for this job, or it was discovered that he fits the psychological profile, or perhaps, like Odysseus, the fates have tied him to this mast and he now awaits the arrival of the harpies.

I am not sure whether I should pray for him, or to him, and shall have to meditate on that.

(P.S. The box of books was returned to me, after my speaking engagements, having been shipped off to O'Hare Airport in Chicago before my first cup of coffee in the early morning, never ever having touched down in Denver. It is part of Riley's destiny that, as to the outcome of my story, as with all the others, he will remain, forever, without a clue.)

The Education of John Woolman

12th day, 6th month, and first of week. (1763) It being a rainy day we continued in our tent, and here I was led to think of the nature of the exercise which hath attended me. Love was the first motion, and then a concern arose to spend some time with the Indians, that I might feel and understand their life and the spirit they live in, if haply I might receive some instruction from them, or they be in any degree helped forward by my following the leadings of Truth among them. And as it pleased the Lord to make way for my going at a time when the troubles of war were increasing, and by reason of much wet weather travelling was more difficult than usual at that season, I looked upon it as a more favorable opportunity to season my mind and bring me into a near sympathy with them.

—John Woolman, *The Journal*

So writes the 18th Century Quaker John Woolman on his way to meet with the Indians of Wyalusing in the north central part of Pennsylvania in the middle of what we now call the French and Indian War. It is difficult at this distance to comprehend what a journey of this kind must have been like in 1763. For much of the 20-day period of travel, there were no roads and no maps. Intermittent rumors of battles, of scalps being taken, and villages and forts being razed to the ground met Woolman along the way. His wife greets the news of his decision to go "with a good degree of resignation."

It wasn't his only trip, or his last. From his first two-week excursion from his home in southern New Jersey in 1743 at the age of 23, to his voyage to England and subsequent death in 1772, Woolman traveled, mostly on foot, the length and breadth of the American colonies. For much of this time, he was a one-man abolitionist movement (later to be joined by his fellow Quaker Anthony Benezet and other members of the Religious Society of Friends), reasoning, cajoling, and praying with Friends to free their slaves, not only because of the evil done to the enslaved—as clear as he was on that subject—but as much because of slavery's negative social and spiritual impacts upon the slaveowners themselves. Woolman would refuse to stay in homes where slaves where kept, or, where he had to, would pay the slaves for their services. By 1761, he gave up the wearing of dyed clothing, both because they represented what he would call a 'superfluity', and because the dyes were made from indigo, a product of slave labor. We can see him in his gray, undyed hat and gray coat and trousers, sitting in Meeting on Sunday (or "First Day", as Friends call it) among a sea of "Quaker Blue". Within 15 years the blue would be gone: by the time of the American Revolution, virtually all Quakers had freed their slaves, with most voluntarily providing what in today's parlance would be called "reparations".

What is startling to the modern reader about the reflections of Woolman's travels as found in his *Journal*, and especially one raised on "literature", are their interiority. There are no descriptions of place, no scenery, and little of people. There are no birds, no flowers, no trees (somewhat surprisingly, given that Woolman made part of his meager living as an orchardist.) There are no smells, and no colors (not even of the dye he decides to abjure). There is reference to taste, that of sugars, and his resolution to "decline to gratify" his palate with them because they are the product of slave labor in the West Indies. There are, however, many reflections upon the weather, as it has direct bearing on his ability to travel. Like his contemporary and publisher Benjamin Franklin, with whose *Autobiography* the *Journal* is often compared, what is important for Woolman is the record of his meditations as he goes forth on his temporal and spiritual excursions.

Woolman's *Journal* reveals a keen moral awareness of the issues behind the French and Indian War. He understands that those who have gone out to live upon the western frontier have often done so to escape the usurious rents set by wealthy landowners who have themselves forsaken "honest employment", only to settle on land they have not purchased, or to procure a living by selling rum to the natives. Perceiving that the Indians have engaged in hard travel and engendered much fatigue in hunting for skins and furs, he emphasizes that they often sell their wares low to acquire more rum, after which "they suffer for want of the necessaries of life", and "are angry with those who for the sake of gain took advantage of their weakness." Woolman notes that the extending of English settlements means that, for the Indians, "those wild beasts they chiefly depend on for their subsistence are not so plenty as they were," and, having been driven back by force, now have to pass over mountains, swamps, and barren deserts to bring their skins and furs to trade. And this in turn, leads him, as he is walking, to be "led into a close, laborious inquiry whether I, as an individual, kept clear from all things which tended to stir up or were connected with war, whether in this land or Africa, and my heart was deeply concerned in future I might be in all things keep steadily to the pure Truth."

Woolman is not without physical fears, and as he travels in the face of perils, wonders whether he continues on as a matter of false pride:

> In this grand distress I grew jealous of myself, lest the desire of reputation as a man firmly settled to persevere through dangers, or the fear of disgrace arising on my returning without performing the visits, might have some place in me.

He writes that he is not fearful of being killed by the Indians, for God in His mercy would care for him. But he does fear being taken captive for, he being of "tender constitution", they "might demand service of me beyond what I could well bear." As bereft as the *Journal* is of physical colors, textures, and tastes, and, it is worth adding, of humor, so is it a veritable panoply of psychological and spiritual shadows and shadings. Here, his palette is unstinting.

And yet, to what end this journey? Woolman is traveling, for him rather uniquely, with exquisitely little in the way of an agenda. There are no Quaker gatherings to frequent or to preach at, no widows to comfort, no slaveowners in need of convincement, no committee meetings to attend to compose epistles against the payment of war taxes, no plan of mediation between warring parties to negotiate or implement, no rare worldly commerce for him to enter upon. Here, there is neither the practicality of a Franklin (or, in his own way, of Woolman himself) nor a precursor of modern tourism. He goes, simply and straightforwardly, to meet with total strangers, of customs and language unknown to him, to understand their life and spirit, to receive instruction of them, and share of himself. Love being the first motion that animates his spirit, there is nothing of greater import—neither wife nor family, neither employment nor commitments to his religious community, not even his crusade against slavery—for him to attend to.

When he arrives, and now finding himself in the company of a Moravian evangelical missionary, Woolman presents a certificate to the Indians from his Friends Meeting regarding his good conduct and his concern. He indicates that he has no intention of preaching or converting, or holding any special sessions, but simply asks for permission to attend their meetings and to speak "when love engaged me thereto." At one of these meetings, feeling his "mind covered with the spirit of prayer", he asks the interpreters (who seem from what we can tell to be somewhat bewildered and "none of them quite perfect in the English and Delaware tongue"), not to interpret, for he "believed that if I prayed right he (God) would hear me". At the rise of the meeting, one of the Indians, Papunehang by name, says of Woolman's message to one of the interpreters who has been silent the entire time, "I love to feel where words come from."

And that, essentially, is all. He returns to his home (and later wanderings), having "so often been confirmed in a belief that whatever the Lord might be pleased to allot for me would work for good, I was careful lest I should admit any degree of selfishness in being glad overmuch..." He has met "that of God" (in the language of Friends) in those who otherwise might be most alien to him, befriended them, and is enlarged as a result, "having laboured to improve by those trials in such a manner as my gracious Father and Protector intends for me."

* * * * *

It is good for thee to dwell deep that thou mayest feel and understand the spirits of people.

—John Woolman, *The Journal*

Love is the first motion, as every mother of a newborn (and every father, if but at greater distance) knows. It is both a miracle and a mystery, this love. After all, up until now, the child-to-be has, for the most part, been a source of discomfort and, mostly recently, pain. If pregnancy was not a celebrated part of our cultural experience (and, sadly, less celebrated all the time), it would be difficult to perceive it as a gift, rather than a source of foreboding and, perhaps, woe. (And, until the last century, probably as often woe as occasion for thanksgiving.)

This lump of less-than-firm protoplasm of seemingly indistinct intelligence hardly seems a fitting object of our approbation. We speak of its appearance among us in pounds and ounces, inches and fractions, the time of the lying-in, the drugs necessary to facilitate its arrival, forcibly ejected or (ever-more commonly) violently yanked from its warm, dark, sheltered, comfortable solitude.

The newborn is nothing if not "otherness" personified. It is unbounded by language or tradition. It does not walk with us, converse with us, share our stories, sing our songs, laugh at our jokes. But somehow, somewhere, beyond the reach of the trappings of culture, we have learned, from a place beyond teaching, to see ourselves in this other, and by such seeing have been motioned to love. Culture has bent itself to this celebration, too, in as many ways as cultures have engaged to express themselves. For it is in embracing this otherness, by drawing it into ourselves (even, in this case, having first physically expelled it), that we grow.

Every friend and every enemy was a newborn once, and a child. Every president and maharajah, every singer and seer, every poet and painter, every holy man, secretary, soldier, and garbage man, every prostitute and drug addict, con artist and saint, voyager and cripple, millionaire and salesman, hunter, patriarch, pimp, architect, and pea farmer, every fisherman and nurse, pirate and foundling, insurance broker and snake charmer, ax murderer and prince is part of this never-ending round of birth and birthing.

They are all part of our circle. This is not always a comfortable truth, or a comforting one. Some we would perhaps desire to banish from recognition as part of our species.

But banishment is not an option. For in our own little ways, in ways which we may not be willing to admit to ourselves except in the middle of sleepless nights or in the circle of dreams, we partake of all of them. They are part of who we are as human beings, and we are drawn to them, as much as we might think at times that we would prefer otherwise, like iron filings to magnet. And by them, even in our rejection of them, we are enlarged, or at the very least changed.

We are all Indians to each other.

* * * * *

I love to feel where words come from.

Long before the words make any sense to the infant (or so we believe), she is drawn to them. They entertain relationship, first to the mother, then perhaps to a father and siblings, or a great aunt. There is sense before sensibility, or upon which the latter depends, the sense-idea that others are knowable, and help form the ground upon which we come to know ourselves.

There likely is no self to speak of, no less to think on, without there being others, just as it is unlikely that there can be such a thing as thought that cannot be spoken. Nature has built nurture into the core of our very beings. The nurturing place where words come from is nature herself (and one can capitalize Nature if one so chooses.) For whatever purpose upon the earth we are created, we are not amoebae who can simply subdivide, and then go our separate ways. It just doesn't work that way.

And so even before our children know what the words mean (or so we believe), they know they come from a place, loci of safety and security, or of anger or hazard, some as welcoming, others (and hopefully there are few) of danger.

From here they go out to meet the world, to take it in, make sensibility of sense, build a more complete picture, give it form and language, furnish their own mental and physical world, and inhabit it as themselves. This process is what we grace with the word *learning*.

* * * * *

Five years before his visit with the Indians, John Woolman wrote an essay related to education, understood in its narrower sense of the term. It was first published in 1758 as part of a series of four essays: "Considerations on Pure Wisdom, and Human Policy; on Labor; on Schools; and on The Right Use of the Lord's Outward Gifts". It was last published in 1922 (though it is now published here for the first time in more than 80 years, in the Appendix.) Given the holistic, all-encompassing frame of Woolman's mind, schools are inseparable from these other objects of his concern. To think clearly about education, one must view it in the context of wisdom, human policy, labor, and how we best go about ordering our use of resources—both natural and human—and our consciousness as well.

"On Schools" is only six paragraphs long, and within a span of just over 900 words, and in the quaint but trenchant language of 18th Century Quakerism, Woolman provides both a framework for a critique of the next 250 years in the development of American education, and an entire basis for an alternative to it. Indeed, as a labor to unfold its wisdom, it is difficult to forego the temptation to quote it in full!

Woolman begins, "To encourage children to do things with a view to get praise of men appears an obstruction to their being inwardly acquainted with the spirit of truth." Woolman accepts the possibility that in encouraging the love of praise, children may sometimes learn things faster than they otherwise would, but to do so is to neglect the very purposes of education:

That Divine light which enlightens all men, does, I believe, often shine in the minds of children very early; and humbly to wait for wisdom that our conduct towards them may tend to forward their acquaintance with it, and strengthen them in obedience thereto, appears to me to be a duty on us all.

The danger is not that children will not learn, but that depending upon praise may set a life pattern that obstructs a commitment to what really matters.

Teachers are Woolman's next object of concern. The standard for teachers has to be higher than for the average citizen, with frame of mind rightly prepared so as to not ensnare a child, not only by their conduct but by their methods of teaching, in "the wisdom of the world":

It is a lovely sight to behold innocent children; and when they are sent to schools where their tender minds are in imminent danger of being led astray by tutors, who do not live a self-denying life, or by the conversation of such children as do not live in innocence, it is a case much to be lamented.

Sometimes, of course, it is not the fault of the teacher per se, but simply that he

hath charge of too many, and his thoughts and time are so much employed in the outward affairs of his school, that he does not so weightily attend to the spirits and conduct of each individual, as to be enabled to administer rightly to all in due season; through such omission, he not only suffers as to the state of his own mind, but the minds of his children are in danger of suffering also.

For when too great a number are committed to a single teacher, "and he, through much cumber, omits a careful attention to the minds of his scholars, there is danger of disorders increasing among them, until they grow too strong to be easily remedied." For regardless of how "education" is conducted, unless one believes in something like a "hundredth monkey" theory—whereby the consciousness of many directly forms the consciousness of the individual—learning happens one child at a time. Woolman's remedy is a simple one, that more time be spent by parents, and by tutors in school "in weightily attending to the spirits and inclination of children." For this is our responsibility:

To watch the spirits of children, to nurture them in gospel love, and labor to help them against that which would mar the beauty of their minds, is a debt we owe them; and a faithful performance of our duty not only tends to their lasting benefit, and to our own peace, but also renders their company agreeable to us.

* * * * *

In learning, *we meet up with and remake ourselves.* We take in from the outside, we reorganize, we test for coherence, for consistency, for agreement with that which we think we already know, and create anew. Every time we learn something new our entire brain-mind is reorganized, fresh connections established, and others fall by the wayside. Physicians make use of this fact in the rehabilitation of stroke victims. This in-built capacity for *cortical reorganization* makes it possible to take advantage of functional and structural neuronal plasticity. This plasticity is greatest, of course, among children. The great truth here is that habits of mind are both physiological and psychological facts.

And that's why such care must be taken in the education of children. Often, it is the context of education, rather than its content, which makes up the bulk of learning, and through which habits of mind sink into our unconscious. Children are resilient—they are made that way—but they are not invulnerable. Once you accept as true that it is possible to beat a child into learning her times tables but that then she is likely to associate math with pain and humiliation for the remainder of her life, the rest is simply a matter of degree. Make children understand through experience that learning is associated with boredom on the one hand or embarrassment on the other and you "have marred the beauty of their minds." Teach a child that learning is bound up with relentless interrogation and regurgitation on demand, and her untended powers of discovery will atrophy. Teach the musical child that singing happens only on alternate Thursdays when the music teacher makes her appearance, and she will learn to devalue what could be her greatest gift. Teach the physically active child that learning only takes place when he remains in his little chair behind the little desk, and that pharmacological agents are the only way to *help* him do so, and he will believe that he is sick, and was born that way. Label a "late reader" a "slow learner", and you have blighted her joyous and unsettling journey into competence and self-understanding. Praise children unstintingly and only for right answers, and, in search of further praise, they are less likely to make use of their capacities of inquisitiveness. Tell a child repeatedly that "now is not a good time for questions", and eventually he will have fewer of them. Once you have either praised or beaten, bullied or manipulated, bribed or humiliated, goldstarred or drugged or just plain ignored a child into habits of unthinking compliance or unmindful submission, it is that much more difficult for her to grow out of them, to find and make use of 'more favorable opportunities to season her mind'.

Our children are going off to meet the Indians—and everyone and everything else. They will pass over mountains, swamps, and barren deserts, occasionally picking up a handful of pebbles and stuffing them into their pockets, sometimes just staring upwards at the boundless expanse of stars and sky. Everything they need for this journey was given to them upon creation, and to us to outfit them properly.

Trust in your love for your children, even as (if you are of a religious frame of mind) you trust in the love of the Great Creator for you. If you are not of a religious persuasion, trust in your love for your children as an evolutionary truth, a love which is the impetus for the future progress of the species. And if neither of these views speaks to your condition, trust in your love for your children because, even with the seeming burden of an entire culture—Woolman's "wisdom of the world—weighing upon you, you simply know in your heart that it is right.

Dwell deep that thou mayest feel and understand the spirits of children.

And, while you're at it, please give them a big hug for me.

* * * * *

The best modern in-print edition of Woolman's works is *The Journal and Major Essays of John Woolman*, edited by Phillips P. Moulton (Richmond, IN: Friends United Press, 1989). I have given away more copies than I care to remember. Unfortunately, some of the best, most dynamic instances of Woolman's writing are contained in essays not found here, including "Considerations on Pure Wisdom, and Human Policy." For these, one must seek out the 1922 edition of Woolman's works, edited by Amelia Mott Gummere.

For a contemporary explication of Woolman's faith and practice, with suggestions of how it might be applied in the modern world, I heartily recommend *A Near Sympathy: The Timeless Wisdom of John Woolman* by Earlham College Professor of Religion Michael Birkel (Richmond, IN: Friends United Press, 2003).

Now that I have mentioned Earlham College, for homeschooling families seeking to provide their teenagers with a pre-taste of the college experience, I want to put in a plug for Earlham's Explore-A-College. It takes place for two weeks every summer, and I know many homeschooled kids, both Friends and not, who come back with glowing reports. It draws on a national and even international student base. Students get to live in the dorms, and to live and build community with each other, study with very fine faculty, and participate in activities both athletic and artistic. There is also significant financial aid for families in need of it. Check it out at www.earlham.edu/~eac/

Finally, for those with children ages 10-18 seeking a non-competitive summer music experience, I can give no higher recommendation than to Friends Music Camp in Barnesville, Ohio. Open to Friends and non-Friends alike, only a year of prior musical experience is required, and I find it hard to imagine that a child will find a more supportive music adventure, one run in the spirit of a Quaker community. www.quaker.org/friends-music-camp/

Poetry in Motion

Yeow! I'm sore!

I just got home from my Jazzercise class at the city parks and recreation center, and have tumbled into my writing chair. Don't laugh—it's not funny! (yet!) I haven't so far managed to say anything at all witty, and my bones and muscles don't feel amused.

All right, it is an entertaining sight. Me and 35 sweaty women. Big ones and little ones. Fat ones and skinny ones and svelte ones and odd-shaped ones. Young ones and…young-at-hearts. One or two pregnant. (I, of course, am the oddest shaped of all!) They've decided I'm just one of the girls. Good thing, too, because I'm not sure how I could deal with it otherwise.

Jazzercise is "a cardio-enhancing combination of dance and exercise." Or at least they tell me it is cardio-enhancing—at the moment, I'm not sure I could find a pulse. There are some fine dancers in the class who are also in great shape. There are some folks in great shape who don't dance worth beans. There are also some out-of-shape dancers. Then there is the back row. I'm in the back row. We don't dance too good (I'm being kind), and after about 20 minutes, we have trouble lifting our feet.

There are two women, both in their 60s I think, who have been doing this three times a week for 20 years. Sigh. I can't imagine doing this for 20 years. I'll have to push myself to go back on Thursday. One day at a time. That's why I bought the big 16-session pass. I'm a cheapskate, and having spent the dough in advance, there's no way I'm not going to get my money's worth, even if I die in the attempt. "We Shall Overcome," I keep wanting to sing after each session.

Sadly, the music isn't jazz. Up-tempo disco mostly, the kind I deliberately missed the polyester years to avoid. The high point is some of the songs from "Flashdance" (no Jennifer Beals anywhere in the vicinity); then there's assorted "disco-country" (does such a category exist, or did I just make that up? What do you call 'Tanya Tucker'? I am well beyond my range of cultural competence here.) Something called "Irish Techno" (?) My new favorite is an "education" song by a guy named Thomas Dolby, "She Blinded Me with Science":

It's poetry in motion
And when she turned her eyes to me
As deep as any ocean

As sweet as any harmony
She blinded me with science
And failed me in biology.

I don't think I'd ever get into an automobile with someone who played this stuff on the car stereo. But here I am.

I do need to find a way to get some exercise that doesn't involve round things. In my early-to-mid 40s, I used to play full-court basketball three times a week. Don't get the wrong impression: it's not what it seems. I'm short, slow, and can't jump, all three being congenital, which I think means they had to let me play under the Americans with Disabilities Act. I was certainly no worse in my 40s than I was in my 20s, which doesn't say much, and I could hear the cheers of the mythical multitude every time I managed to get a shot off, which was rather rare, or even succeed in running up and down the court twice without gasping for breath. But, alas, the body wouldn't heal fast enough from all the elbows and hip checks, and I had to hang 'em up.

I also liked to play softball. I styled myself a good infielder, with slick hands, and a relatively weak bat. Scrappy! Alack, now when I play catch, I see the ball perfectly up until it gets about two feet away, and then I lose it. More often than not, the ball bounces off the heel of the glove…or worse. Softball has simply become too hazardous.

And so, at least for the present, it's Jazzercise. I'd be hard-pressed to say I actually like it, but for now, I can get by with a detached and sweaty amusement, and there's no question me and the girls get quite a workout. The instructor, who never seems to approach even moist (though I can't see that well from where I sweat), calls out steps and counts, but I have no idea what the steps are called or what she is counting. And she can talk and dance and bend and sway and jump all at the same time! She follows baseball, and Barry Bonds. Doesn't care for Paris Hilton. ("Skankoid," she says.) I mostly "copy" (all right—that's a little euphemistic), and smile a bunch and sweat a lot. She comments that I'm a really happy guy. I'm trying to convince myself that I am, or at least that I can talk myself into it. I look around. We are *all* smiling. We are poetry in motion! And the gym floor moves.

So what do we have to teach the kids so that they can live to be 105? I don't think I should be the one to ask, as my particular genetic inheritance makes the possibility of such an accomplishment very doubtful. Still, I always enjoy the advice passed down in the newspaper by those who have managed this particular feat of longevity. You know, "Smoke a cigar after dinner every night; drink two shots of vodka before lunch; sing in the bathtub; always vote for the challenger; don't read depressing newspaper stories, etc., etc." (I've discovered you can even scramble them: "Smoke a cigar in the bathtub every night; drink two shots of vodka after reading a depressing newspaper story; always vote before lunch....")

Don't preach. Let your kids see you taking good care of yourself. Or at least look like you're trying. Eat right, and enjoy that extra piece of cheesecake. Stay in shape (what shape is yet to be determined; but I'm clearly more "well-rounded" than I used to be.) Imbibe a little if you like, or abstain, but don't make a big deal about it either way. Make walking to the supermarket, rather than driving, a religious observance. Sleep occasionally. Do something that feeds your soul, and do something that feeds other people's. Know at least a few of your neighbors. Always stretch beyond your comfort zone. If you already know how to country line-dance, learn to tango. Live with intention.

Don't sweat the small stuff. That's what the Jazzercise class is for, and, if you're like me, you'll forget it every time you try to raise your left knee.

* * * * *

P.S. I am offering $5.00 off any of my other books to any homeschooling parent of the masculine persuasion who sends me a receipt from having attended a Jazzercise class. I need a support group.

Unspelling™

I took the day off from work. I was feeling quite under the weather (and we have *a lot* of weather where I live!) I settled myself into my ten-dollar, coffee-stained Salvation Army recliner (being brown to begin with among its saving graces), tea in hand (encupped, of course), two dogs happily yawning at my feet, and began to channel surf. Yes, guilty as charged. I throw myself on the mercy of the court, my only mitigating circumstance being that my eyes have declined to the point that it is now difficult to read unless I am in tip-top physical condition.

Switch to ESPN. I am in luck! Well, maybe. No Gaelic stone-tossing, or heavyweight Strong Man auto-pulling. Today is the National Spelling Bee! I probably would have preferred college women's softball or trial runs for the Iditarod, but this promises to be different.

It is scheduled for five hours (as long as two Montana State football games!) It will never in my affections surpass Olympic curling (wish I could get those guys with brooms to come to my house! and why isn't this sport co-ed, inquiring minds want to know?) or singles synchronized swimming, but it is deadly addictive. In exchange for a single $10,000 college scholarship, parents and schools across the entire United States have united in this cruel effort to uncover their children's spelling deficits. ESPN rakes in hundreds of thousands of dollars in advertising revenue on the assumption that I am more likely to purchase golfing shoes (I HATE golf!) or use "Duz" ("May I have the language of origin, please?") to take care of those nasty grass stains if they can just keep me glued for the next five hours to my recliner. The advertisers are probing for my deficits as well. Well, here I am.

Don't get me wrong now: I've taken as much delight in homeschoolers' recent monopoly of the National Spelling Bee as the next homeschooler, and have been just as outraged by official attempts to limit our kids' participation. But, as a *Washington Post* staff writer recently wrote, this really is "an archaic exercise in brutality". The idea behind the Spelling Bee is that one is supposed to keep one's deficit hidden as long as possible, while hundreds of other prepubescent geeks (having been one myself, I remember the feeling) reveal their fatal flaws and are banished ignominiously from the island. No team spirit here; there definitely will not be any bug-swallowing for the good of the group. And most assuredly there are not two Miss Spelling Bee North Carolinas.

No, once the fatal flaw is revealed, as in Survivor II, one has to leave, alone, returning, with any luck, to a more comfortable surround. It's one giant 'sudden death' playoff. So there it is, five hours of morbidly watching kids fail!

But not only that, for as the game progresses, the words get harder and harder, and, progressively, less and less useful. Consider how many times you have utilized any of the following words in your writing or speech in the past several decades: *xanthosis*; *vivisepulture*; *euonym*; *chiaroscurist*; *logorrhea*; *demarche*; *succedanaeum*; *prospicience*. These were the final words in each of the last eight National Spelling Bees. (I would note that my spellchecker highlights all but one of them as misspelled. Now going for one million dollars, can you tell us which one? And for ten million: use all eight in a single, meaningful sentence—you have 60 seconds. Ready?) (I just did: "The following words—xanthosis, vivisepulture, etc., etc.—never appear together in an English sentence." Applause!) One word you don't see on this list is *triskaidekaphobia*, a word that has probably resulted in more banishments than any other. (Meaning? Fear of the number 13!) Meera, having just mastered *triskaidekaphobia*, has just downloaded a list of 276 other *phobia* words, and is now busy memorizing.

I finally managed to turn it off. There! That wasn't so bad, was it? Next time, scanning the globe for the world of sport, there are a host of other events I'd prefer to see (I hope the folks at ESPN are reading this), such as the Great Bathtub Race of Nome, Alaska (www.nomenugget.com), the World Championship Rotary Tiller Race (which, as *everyone* knows, is part of the PurpleHull Pea Festival of Emerson, Arkansas (www.purplehull. com), or the Extreme Ironing World Championships, last held in Munich (www.extremeironing.com). I also might express a preference for the World Bog-Snorkeling Championships, "run" (?) every August in Llanwrtyd (love the spelling), Wales, or the Punkin Chunkin World Championships (www.punkinchunkin.com) held in Rehoboth, Delaware. (There are college scholarships attached to this one!) To be sure, none of these will outdo my predilection for the Cooper Hill Annual Cheese Rolling and Wake (www. cheese-rolling.co.uk), a favorite of the BBC and an event known through documentary evidence to be at least 200 years old, and which may date back as far as pre-Arthurian Britain. If there are advertisers, there is sure to be an audience, or is it the other way around? I think there is likely a lot less violence associated with these (with the possible exception of Extreme Ironing) than with word-flaying.

Really, I guess it's not too terrible to have a Little League World Series of Spelling. Some of our children will never make it as shortstops, and, if they like competition and arcane words, this is their chance for 15 minutes of fame.

But for most of our kids, this is not a good, or even particularly enjoyable way to advance the spelling skill. As enthusiastic as we may be, some of them are less than enthusiastic in learning about Latin and Greek roots, terms for obscure medical diagnoses, or even spending a lot of time with the dictionary.

And they shouldn't have to. For many children, with lots of good reading and good conversation that allows them to expand their conceptual horizons, spelling takes care of itself. In terms of vocabulary, research has shown that the average five-year-old child (if there is such a thing as an "average" child) knows approximately 10,000 words. She will gain another 2,000-3,000 words a year until her vocabulary at age 18 will be approximately 40,000. And again, with more good reading and good conversation, it will just keep growing. (The same studies show that in classrooms, children are formally introduced to no more than 300-500 words a year, and since they may already have known about half of them before being "taught", they are obviously getting well more than three-quarters of them from somewhere else!)

They learn to spell them, too. Some simply remember words after seeing them in print. Others draw phonemic analogies from other words they have heard or seen, and that works about 90% of the time. Still others pick it up through the computer spellchecker.

Parents who participated in spelling bees as children have repeatedly given me a tidbit that I think we can put to good use. They always remember the word that stumped them in the childhood spelling bee, and now (unlike so many other words) always spell it correctly (although I have also met one person who is permanently blocked from ever feeling that she can spell this particular word), even as they remember the shame and embarrassment of having been banished from the island. So I began to ask myself whether there might be a way of making use of this insight, without the shame, embarrassment, and banishment that characterized the competition.

And I've found one! I've now used it with a dozens of kids ages 7 to 15 (adults, too), and it works. They always want to do more of it. It's a game I've given the name Unspelling™.

Unspelling™ works like this: one person picks a source word. Then, in turn, each of the players must spell this word incorrectly, but with a basis in a sound-analogy with the way another word (or words) is correctly spelled. If challenged, she must produce that word. If you run out of spellings, if you repeat a previous Unspelling™, *or if you spell the word correctly*, you're out. The first few times you play, it is easier to write the Unspelling™ words on a blackboard or piece of butcher paper hung on the wall, but doing it without aid of writing will enhance memory development.

Example: the Unspelling™ source word is "phonics".

phonix	fonix	fonics	fonicks
phonicks	foknicks	phoknicks	foknics
phoknics	phanics	fanics	phanix
fanix	phanicks	fanicks	phaknicks
faknicks	faknics	phaknics	fonnics
phonics	phonnix	fonnix	fonnicks
phonnicks	fannics	phonnicks	phannics
phannicks	fannicks		

One could add words beginning with "pf" as in "pfennig" (German currency, but used in English, it appears in the dictionary.) (And if one decides to allow analogies with Polish or Slavic proper names, the list might expand to include words ending in "icz".)

Get the idea? A favorite Unspelling™ source word of mine is "weighty" (which has among the strangest *correct* spellings). Just to get started:

waytee	wheytea	whaytea	weitie
whaytie	wayttie	waittea	weightea
etc.			

You can see that this particular Unspelling™ source word would make for a very long list!

The benefits of Unspelling™ are obvious, or at least they are to me. First of all, once kicked out of the game for spelling a word correctly, it will never be forgotten. Secondly, players come away with an expanded sense of the phonetic possibilities of the language, which will help both with future spelling questions, and in figuring out pronunciation from written sources.

More important than either of these, Unspelling™ is fun! A lot more fun than the spelling bee, or so every kid who has ever tried it has told me. Probably more fun than Extreme Ironing or Bog-Snorkeling (at least for many), though I doubt it can measure up with the Cheese Rolling. ESPN— are you there? We are almost ready for prime time!

A Long Way Since Yo-Yos

When it comes to video games, I am agnostic. Also, as shall eventually become clear, uncomfortable. But I'm pleased by the opportunity to get around to this essay, as I think it will contain a little something to get virtually everyone's dander up. A bit of controversy can go a long way in my book, and this is, after all, my book (and yours, too, I hope, if you've paid for it.)

Yes, I have read it all: exposure to video games can fry juvenile brain cells, poach prepubescent eyeballs, and turn our otherwise angelic Johnnies and Susies into incipient ax murderers, awaiting just the right moment to unleash their preprogrammed rage. At best, they are squandering valuable time and "wasting potential" that could have been better spent studying ancient Chaldean, learning country tap dancing, or enhancing their social skills, perhaps by teasing their big sisters.

Now, mind you, I don't discount these sinister possibilities. It's just, perhaps, that I have become a bit jaded. When I was growing up (as opposed to out) back in the Dark Ages, research had proven conclusively that ballpoint pens would ruin our hands (or was it "hand"?), and wearing sneakers for more than one hour a day was definitively known to destroy our feet. Conceivably, by some strange genetic anomaly, my appendages still seem to work, though my handwriting—if it could be called that—well, enough said, and, despite my Keds (for a great history of sneakers, go to Charlie's Sneaker Pages—http://sneakers.pair.com), I never was able run or jump worth beans, or get beyond the two-hand set-shot. If it wasn't for ballpoint pens and canvas high-tops, who knows where I'd be today?

Whatever you happen to think about video games (and their computer-oriented brethren), you have to agree that the game designers, and the child and behavioral psychologists that advise them, are absolutely brilliant! I mean, they can take young 'uns who would otherwise be diagnosed with ADHD or some such (or actually already are) and, without resort to a single pharmacological agent, enable them to sit and interact with rapt attention for hours on end, become fixated on goals and the strategies necessary to accomplish them, approach these strategies with creativity and intelligence, achieve their missions, and move right on to the next ones, learning all the time.

We've come a long way since yo-yos, baby. And though I do not have much direct experience with them, I think it is relatively easy to understand the needs the games serve so well. The child learns to feel in control, unself-conscious, oblivious to emotional problems or external demands, not dependent upon others, neither bored nor frustrated, and, increasingly, competent. Whew, that's quite a list!

It is interesting that when I speak with mothers (it is almost always mom who seems to be most worried about it, and with whom I am more likely to share my pacifist DNA), they often tell me that they can't fathom what their kids see in the video games. Now I readily admit to being perhaps more squeamish than is "manly". But having children engaged in the genial art of human evisceration—even of the virtual variety—does not strike me as a particularly wholesome or salutary activity. However, I note that youth violence rates have steadily declined as violent video games have become more widespread; maybe some of the potential pubescent psychopaths—not especially affected by video games one way or the other—are spending more of their time indoors? What is more striking to me is that it is very rare to find parents actually trying to ascertain what exactly it is that has caught their kids between its teeth and refuses to let go. I can count on one hand the number of mothers I have met (homeschooling or otherwise) who have put in the time and energy to learn the video games that their little darlings play, and learned them well enough to experience the feeling of competence and "flow" that can come from mastering them. Not surprisingly, ignorance breeds fear. (Important note: Please don't take up this challenge while the dear boy is around. He'll never forgive me for having instigated your invasion of his turf!)

If you watch the kids "playing" at this activity, it becomes quickly obvious that they are not "vegging out". On the contrary, they are alert and alive, in ways that many rarely experience otherwise. For they are learning, only without mom (or the schoolteacher) spying over their shoulders "testing" them for right answers. No one is checking on their proficiency, forcing them to repeat things again and again, interrupting them, insisting on the single denotative meaning of an activity. And, played with their friends, they can critique, instruct, analyze, and review—*socialize*—without any fear that it will become part of their "permanent record", either in the bowels of the local middle school, or in dad's indelible brain. Video games allow them a sense of independence they may rarely experience in their academic or even non-academic lives.

No "down" time, this. On the contrary, where video games differ from "normal" "play" time (wow, are these terms loaded!) is in their relentless goal orientation. Small goals set and small goals met lead to larger ones, new puzzles posed and new ones solved, in an endless round of increasing difficulty and expanding mastery. No wonder some kids are so insistent on defending this territory!

When I was growing up, there were social activities where I was able to experience this flow and, especially, to learn, in either academic or non-academic pursuits. Stickball remains my favorite example, where I learned and experienced competency—goals set and goals met—without any adult supervision whatsoever.

As it turns out, my kids don't play video games. They found other "spaces" at an early age where they were able to learn in freedom without us peering over their shoulders. Meera spends five hours a day in the gym (my wife Ellen and I are both geeky), plays the piano for at least two hours a day (neither Ellen nor I play a note), and spends maybe an hour a day in something remotely resembling academics. She has a new series of relationships with adults through whom she is learning about politics and religion in the Middle East, peacemaking, modern jazz theory, and the history and science behind polio. Pointedly, none of these activities include us (or didn't until recently; see "Meera's New Friends.")

Aliyah from an early age would spend two hours a day in "nature", either walking in the woods, or weaving bark baskets, or some such (I'm from New York City and Ellen's from Washington, DC, so enough said), compose music for an hour or so, play her oboe or violin, teach herself Latin. Since neither Ellen nor I could "supervise" any of these activities, Aliyah had all kinds of space to learn in freedom. In short, both of my kids have been blessed with the psychological space enabled by their parents' ignorance, coupled with our commitment to helping them find new challenges and then getting out of the way.

The point is that the video game folks are preying upon children's needs to feel in control, even as they face and then overcome challenges. When your child entreats grandma for a PlayStation II, he is appealing to her, whether he realizes it or not, to buy him a bit of freedom. Regardless of the inherent value of video games or the lack thereof (as you can see, I'm still hedging my bets), learning that freedom is for sale can't really be a good lesson, can it?

All right, my alter ego, now thoroughly confused, is feverishly waving his arms and demanding his turn, and I promised him a chance, even if not equal time. (I do—sometimes—respect my publishers' word limits, if often in the breach.) So here's what he's got to say: Here is an entire industry composed of adults and traded on the stock market manipulating my children to teach them that "pretend" murder is okay. It may ultimately have no effect on the kids, but what does it say about *me*? As my good friend Shelley McCoy zings, "Would it be okay with you if they played at "pretend rape"? What about getting them some "pretend pornography" for Christmas? What does it say about me, and about my society, that pretend rape or pornography is repugnant, but pretend murder is acceptable, when it "improves strategic thinking and hand-eye coordination"? Whatever happened to tennis? Or chess?

You must admit, or at least *I* must, that Mr. Alter has a point. I might justly choose to ban violent video games in my household, as well as violent TV and movies, to make a statement to my kids about *myself* and *my* values, independent of any potential damage the homicidal media might actually cause. If I were confronted with this situation, it might just be one of those family arguments worth having, if only to prepare the kids for the kinds of arguments they might be having with *my* grandchildren a couple of decades from now. I wouldn't mind being remembered as that old fuddy-duddy who actually decided what was good for them and for our family. I mean, after all, *I* made the decision not to send them to school, and parenting is not supposed to be a popularity contest.

Civilizations and cultures have managed to exist without all this prepackaged blood and gore before, and there's no reason why they couldn't again. There's plenty of work for the kids to do, learning to protect the earth, respect other people, and find ways to align themselves with the forces that build healthy communities, rather than tear them apart.

There ARE, praise be, other alternatives. (And Shelley says, if the boys are really, really bored, and want for something to do, you can always teach them to knit.)

subiyay (1944-2005)

Dear Brothers and Sisters –

Hear what I say! Today, I have gone with the people to celebrate the passage of *subiyay* (aka Gerald Bruce Miller) to the spirit world. And I am here to share with you that while *subiyay* may be gone and our hearts are heavy, as he promised us, his breath is still here.

subiyay has for many years been the *vidadad*, the spiritual teacher, of the Skokomish Tribe, some 25 miles from our home. While I have known him in passing for a long time, he only came into our lives in a significant way through the experience of my older daughter Aliyah this past 18 months or so, and it is for her that I must commemorate his life and spirit.

subiyay was born the last of 15 children on the Skokomish Reservation on Puget Sound. He was born at a time when one could still look and see that the trees were many nations and races, and through the languages of these nations all gathered together, he heard the teachings of the tree people, told in a language that was dying even as he was growing up.

Brothers and sisters, *subiyay* was a youth when there was still material to be gathered for the making of the baskets, which he learned from his elders, who are also now gathered on the other side. From them, he learned *uyayeh*—the medicine of the plant people. He learned the secrets of the inner bark of the alder tree, how it can be used as an anti-inflammatory, as a tonic to fight off streptococcal disease, and as a poultice to bring down the itching of a mosquito bite. And he learned of the medicinal qualities of the salmonberry, of the mushrooms that grow on the willow, and of the huckleberry leaf and devil's club that can be used against diabetes, the disease that afflicted *subiyay* for the last 15 years of his life. All of these and more he resurrected and taught to my daughter in his home, and to other people's sons and daughters, as they worked in his garden, or stripped cedar bark, or wove baskets together, or simply sat quietly by the fire.

Subiyay went to schools where they took away TWANA—his language—and his culture, but he was later to understand that it was the way of schools to do the same to the language and culture of other peoples as well. He spent the better part of the rest of life reclaiming them. He was open-hearted with people of all nations, many of whom came to him from all parts of the world, with gifts of their woven rugs and mats and baskets to trade with those of his people.

Brothers and sisters, *subiyay* fought in a war against people whom he came to understand were not his enemy, and with whom he could later sit and share the gifts of food and laughter. He became an actor and playwright, and worked in New York with the director Robert Wilson, actor Sam Shepard, composer Philip Glass, singer Bette Midler, and many others, until the spirit of his ancestors called him home to make baskets with his mother and his aunts, and to teach their making to the children, and to the many who came to stay. And when he taught, he burned the sacred scents, for he had learned that when one smells the sacred scents, one remembers the teachings. He knew many dances, and the stories of the people, some of which would require several risings and settings of the sun to tell.

Brothers and sisters, *subiyay* taught whomever came to learn, for he understood that his immortality lay in the teachings he would leave behind, and in that way become part of the history of the people. He did not look to the skin color of those who came, and treated rich and poor the same, those quick of speech and those slow of tongue, for, he taught, there is no time for division. He was proudest of being a teacher of teachers, those who will pass it on. And so, though our hearts are heavy, we should not mourn, for *subiyay* has left behind many teachers.

Brothers and sisters, as we are gathered together today, many from afar and many from close by, seated by the woodstoves in the sacred smokehouse, we celebrate the beginning of *subiyay's* new journey with the four gifts: the gift of the drum, the sound of our mother's beating heart; the gift of song, given to us by the bird people, each of us with her own spirit song, and which allows us to express our hopes and convictions; the gift of dance, which allows us to tell the story of the people; and the gift of spoken language, and with it of memory, to carry the knowledge of the ancestors from the beginning of time and transport it into the future. So hear the beating of the drum, the singing of our songs, dance the journey of the people, and let us tell the tales of *subiyay*'s life, and be mindful of one of his great teachings:

"Don't teach all your children exactly the same thing. If you teach them all the same thing, and in the same way, they will come to believe they do not need each other. And that is no teaching at all."

—February 12, 2005

The Walk

On September 11, 2002, or so it was reported by *The New York Times* (September 19, 2002), a memorial was planned in Jersey City, New Jersey to commemorate the events of September 11th the previous year. As a highlight of a truly fitting tribute to those who had died, at the unveiling of a memorial the organizers planned a release of 80 doves that would soar majestically into the sky against the backdrop of the altered Lower Manhattan skyline.

Only problem was that, when the birds were released, some slammed into the plate-glass windows of the surrounding office buildings. Others plunged directly into the Hudson River. Still others careened into a stunned crowd, who, swatting them away, left the area a confusion of feathers. One perched atop the hardhat of a construction worker who had helped clear Ground Zero. Most bobbed in bewilderment across the stage, never spreading their wings at all.

Seems that finding all the homing pigeons in New Jersey already booked up for the day, the organizers—likely all college graduates and products of the area's public and private schools—went to a Newark poultry market and bought 80 squab, birds that probably had never spent significant time outside their cages.

"These pigeons were supposed to fly," insisted Guy Catrillo, a chief organizer of the 9/11 Memorial Committee. "But," he added philosophically, "without a doubt it beats what could have happened to them...they were soup birds. I like the idea that I helped these squab get a second chance."

The program continued awkwardly, despite the birds. "A lot of people were upset because they didn't want them sitting on their heads," said Nuria Almeida, who had come to attend the ceremony with a friend.

The fate of many of the squab is unknown, though some were taken to area animal hospitals. "I saw one today who lives by a hotdog cart," noted Mr. Catrillo several days later, "and I tried to catch him. But he flew away. Pigeons are natural survivors."

(So, I would only have added—products of public and private schools similar to those attended by the organizers—are we.)

* * * * *

In the evenings, I take my older daughter Aliyah (age 14) for a walk in the local wooded park by the inlet. I think a hundred years ago, they would have called this a "constitutional", though I have yet to find much that is overtly political about it.

In reality, it is she who takes me for the walk. If I were to go myself, I wouldn't see much. Oh, there would be trees enough and plants enough, and an occasional mushroom colony on a fallen log, but truly I wouldn't *see* much. I might espy a robin or two, and in the undergrowth, I'd perceive movement suggesting a brown-breasted leaf-wiggling wren (I know enough to know that wrens are to be found down low), and, high above, I might observe movement suggestive of the green-bellied leaf-wiggling warbler. But not much else. The park is like a closed book to me, or one printed in a wholly foreign language.

But when I let her lead, as if by magic an entire world appears. Barn owl adults eye us from low perches attached to great tree trunks, triangulated by three robins, all pointing directly at the moppish hulks. The owl juveniles announce themselves noisily from branches hanging directly over the trail. Juncos are alarmed. Oh, that's what that racket is.

Aliyah walks straight down the path, reaches out her right hand without breaking stride, and pops a moonglow orange berry into her mouth.

"Salmonberry," she says. "Sweet, but with an aftertaste."

I try one, too. Thimbleberries to the left, she points out, unripe.

"When ripened, they'll be like raspberries, but the birds will get them first. But try the huckleberries. The birds don't go for them as much. The bushes won't hold their weight, and the berries are perfectly round and difficult for bird beaks to hold."

Trilliums sit by our feet, and false lilies-of-the-valley, I am informed.

"Where are the true ones?" I ask.

"Not within a couple of hundred miles," she says, "Except in some people's gardens."

She reaches down and plucks a few green leafy things and starts to chew. "Miner's lettuce," she notes, "Better when young."

She hands me a leaf. I wonder whether she does this when I'm not around.

I'm looking at a carved rustic-looking wooden sign, placed maybe 15 inches or so from the ground. "Red elderberry, *Sambucus racemosa*," it reads. I don't see any berries. Just more low-lying, unnamed shrubby green things.

"Look up!" she laughs.

There, right in front of my nose, not five feet away, are sprays of little red berries reaching upwards.

"Can't eat 'em. Elderberries need to be cooked, or they can be poisonous. But they can be quite medicinal."

I remember a song I once heard about elderberry wine. Never drank any, though.

I have been scratched by a bushy thing.

"Watch out for the stinging nettles," she warns.

"A little late," I mutter under my breath.

"There are four antidotes," she giggles, "And you're practically stepping on one of them!"

I look down, and there is a six-inch-long slug just in front of my right toe. I bend down to inspect.

"Mud, bracken fern, elderberry leaves, and slugs. You can rub mud on the scratches, and it will cool them. The fern and the elderberry you make into a poultice."

"What do you do with the slugs, grind them up?"

"No! It's the slug slime. You rub it on and it acts as an anesthetic."

"Doesn't sound very appealing."

"A friend of mine licked one once, and she said it numbed her tongue totally."

That sounded even less appealing. Do rural kids lick slugs to get high? I wouldn't put it past them.

"You can boil the nettles and make tea," she says, "Brings down fever."

We move on. Snails waltz across the path in front of us, as only snails can.

"You know, after a rain, the robins leave the woods and come down to our neighborhood. That's when you see so many of them. Worms are easier picking on a wet, newly mowed lawn."

And then we hear a high-pitched "Screeeeeeech!" And out over the water there is an eagle!

"Not an eagle, Dad, a red-tailed hawk."

"Oh," I stand corrected.

"You know the sound of the solitary eagle you hear at the end of television shows or in commercials? Well, the sound of the eagle is not an eagle. Eagles don't make a screeching sound at all. It's a tape of a red-tailed hawk combined with film of an eagle. The TV people do that, you know."

I have been duly chastened.

And so on and so forth. Walk after walk. On some evenings when she's occupied with music practices or some such, I've taken to driving to the park by myself, and walk up the road to the footpath. Seashells fall from the sky. I look up, and there are two gulls overhead.* And then I realize the shells are not being aimed at me.

Or are they?

Try as I might, I am a stranger here. I *want* to get it. But I'd be lying if I said I did. I am like a French Angora rabbit, bred for a thousand generations indoors. No instincts.

And no real knowledge, either. Oh, I've gotten a little better with the bird names. I've progressed beyond "pigeon, pigeon, pigeon, pigeon, and pigeon," and one day I'll join the Cornell Ornithological Laboratory's Project Pigeon Watch (www.birds.cornell.edu/ppw) to count the number of each of the 28 colorations. Sadly, my storehouse has gotten larger as my eyesight begins to weaken.

But it hasn't really helped much, the naming thing. How do slugs spend their nights and days? When do they sleep? Where do crows go to die? Do plants feel the movement of the planet, or the waxing and waning of the moon?

This is *my* earth, right? So why is it that when I walk here, a place that could never be mistaken for wilderness, I feel I don't belong?

And would it make a difference if I, and the tens of millions of people just like me, *felt* differently? And what, exactly, would that feel like?

---

* A sign has now been placed on my trail by the state Department of Ecology, informing hikers that the aerial bombers are crows, not seagulls. Posting this little tidbit to a homeschooling e-mail list, I immediately received a message back, with several scientic citations, indicating that seagulls—and specifically the variety that makes their home near me—do indeed do the shell-dropping thing, and that it is learned rather than instinctive behavior. (They must see me coming!) It seems the answer to this conundrum lies in the fact that the seagulls only bombard the rocks by the edge of the water, whereas the crows venture fifty yards inland. Learn something new every day! (Now if I could only actually see 'em.)

How do I go about finding out?

* * * * *

Want your kid to turn out as weird as mine? (*Not!* No two kids are ever really alike.) In Washington State we are blessed with a unique institution, the Wilderness Awareness School in Duvall (www.wildernessawareness.org). Founded originally as a high school nature club, through the careful nurturance of its founder Jon Young and a host of native elders including Tony Ten Fingers of the Oglala Lakota People; Gilbert Walking Bull of the Sioux-Lakota, and Chief Jake Swamp of the Iroquois Confederacy, the Wilderness Awareness School offers a full range of programs to children (from ages 8 and up) and adults. The programs are designed to equip individuals with a full set of skills, knowledge, and attitudinal shifts that can be practiced anywhere, from the wilds to the city. These include: naturalist skills; bioregional identity; journaling; ecology and stewardship ethics; wilderness and living skills; hazard identification; natural history; ethnobotany; cultural anthropology and American Indian lore; hands-on research skills; and mentoring. There are full year-round residential programs (in both Washington and Vermont) in which college credits can be earned; weeklong mentoring workshops; wolf-tracking expeditions for teens in Idaho (Aliyah went on one, and didn't open a book for a whole week, which for her must have been a world record!), weekend seminars on understanding the language of birds, and a range of other choices.

But you or your child don't have to travel either. The School offers an extraordinary program called Kamana to help either of you tune in. Get to shake hands with your world and learn its language! Looking for an integrated homeschool curriculum—reading, writing, biology, botany, history, poetry, and social studies all rolled into one? Have one of those kids who can't sit still at the kitchen table but will spend hours exploring the mud puddle? Kamana melds the techniques of modern field ecology with the skills of a native scout. The program takes from one to four years to complete, requires no special equipment other than eyes and ears (and maybe some other sensory organs you never knew you—or your child—had). You could even do it in…Jersey City! At the end of the program, you can count on a walk in the park never being just another walk in the park. And that could make all the difference.

Looking for something for your teen for a week in the summer that is a little bit more domestic? Eva Barr, a homeschooler with two kids, is director of "Flourish: A Summer Experience in Performing Arts & Agriculture". Eva is a founding member of the Lookingglass Theatre Company in Chicago, but is now homesteading at Dreamacres, a 60-acre organic farm in Wyckoff, Minnesota. Flourish faculty include professional artists in music, puppetry, theatre, and dance. Participants live in rustic, timber-framed buildings with minimal electric capacity (all of it solar), and without modern plumbing, and also learn about farming (including plowing with oxen) and alternative technologies. It is very inexpensive, and sounds like a place where one could hardly fail to be inspired to grow. No website, so write Eva at Flourish, RR 1 Box 1243, Wyckoff, MN 55990; or call (507) 352-4255.

Home(schooling)

Some friends of mine started a journal for parents who homeschool gifted kids, and asked me to contribute an article to the inaugural issue. I agreed, as I usually do when I receive an invitation to write (that is, after all, what writers do), and, also as usual, I was swamped at the time. Thankfully, on a trip to deliver a series of talks at a homeschool conference, my plane was delayed. In my experience, plane delays are one of those great and rare gifts. I used the opportunity to meditate on the subject, which I hope will be appreciated, whether you are homeschooling a gifted kid or not, and whether or not you believe in the usefulness of the "g" word.

* * * * *

Reading has become less and less a meditative activity for me as I age. My eyes are not what they used to be. I have no fewer than three pair of reading glasses, all scattered around the house, some in cases, some not. It is not unusual for me to be unable to find any of them. But when I do, and sit down to read, I am always fussing with them. No matter how many times I have the glasses adjusted, they'll slide down my nose, or wiggle from side to side, or be covered with distracting finger marks, or an occasional scratch.

But reading is not meditative for another reason. If the book is any good, my mind will constantly make connections between what I read and other parts of my experience. And, usually, I'll have three or four volumes going at the same time—as I write this, I am somewhat midway through a wonderful translation of a south Indian epic poem *The Cilappatikaram* ("The Tale of the Anklet"), a new history of the Haitian Revolution *Avengers of the New World*, *The Journal and Major Essays of John Woolman* (for probably the tenth time), and a terrific book of political essays by Arundhati Roy. I am also wearing a set of earphones, and am listening to a 1960s recording of *I Pagliacci*, in preparation for a series of opera performance in which I am singing at the end of next month. Sometimes I read for details, sometimes for inspiration, sometimes because I feel under some external obligation, sometimes to feed my head with background information, and sometimes just to escape, though this has become rarer and rarer, even on airplanes. Almost never meditative, though. However, writing sometimes takes on this quality for me now. Garbage in, garbage out? What does that say about that which mediates between them?

My wife goes to Safeco Field to sell hotdogs at Mariners' games to raise money for my younger daughter Meera's gymnastics club. Oh, goody! If I have the evening off, which means I am not at an orchestral or opera rehearsal, got through my jazzercise class, am not ferrying said daughter from place to place, or am not at a meeting or study group organized by my Friends Meeting, chances are I'll take over the family room. I'll turn on the television and tune in to the baseball game and turn off the sound; set up a music stand with a chair in front and take out my violin; put the phone at one end of the couch; open a book I'm reading "for pleasure" next to it; scatter the papers and what-not I am using in preparation for my next book; open the laptop to an essay I am working on for one of my magazine columns, and another file which contains the beginnings of a letter to a friend. I may also have an operatic score nearby. The Internet and e-mail connection is in another room, ready for me when I "take a break". I never do this when my long-suffering wife is around; it would drive her even more nuts than I do already. (She is very kind!) I'm in my "elements".

The fact is I cannot remember a time when I wasn't like this. No, I did not and do not have ADHD, even if all my teachers had "ADTD" (Attention Deficit Teaching Disorder—characterized as the inability to focus on any one individual less than 59 inches tall for more than 90 seconds at a time, or manifesting feelings of anxiety or anger when required to do so). I spent 12 years in school fidgeting, allowing my "Globally Gifted Attentions" (GGA) to be applied to whatever was at hand. Yes, I could keep the teachers at arms length by volunteering right answers at selected intervals, enough to ensure their more limited attentions remained focused on the middle of the classroom rather than on the far righthand corner (something good about having a last name that begins with A is that I was often out of the teacher's line of sight.) I'd scribble, and count the number of people who walked up and down the hallway. Sometimes I'd hide a library book in my lap. No music, though, which to this day I deeply regret. I compensated in any way I could for the larger lack of material. More than anything else, I would have just liked to have someone to talk to, and who would have had something to share back. More than anything else, in this sea of seven-year-olds, I was lonely. And I'm now 55 years old, and I'm still angry about it! (And bemused by the fact that there is still a charge in it for me.)

Over the years, in helping my daughters navigate their educational journeys, I have learned the language of learning disabilities, and the emotional ones, the initials of, and scoring algorithms for, the various intelligence tests, the proclivities and learning styles of assorted varieties of gifted children, the legal parlance of accommodation. They are, or at least can be, important elements in the armamentaria of parents of gifted kids as we go out and assist our children in wrestling with the world.

But sometimes our children's needs are in fact a little simpler, a little more "elemental". Knowing this doesn't make their lives any easier, especially in institutional settings, which is why we've helped our kids fly the coop, right? It is good just to be able to articulate it. At bottom, what is it that we really want for our kids? Perhaps, not much more, really, than that they be treated with kindness, and with a healthy dose of respect. A little kindness, for everyone, goes a long way. Respect for the fact that they are both gifted and children, and not necessarily in that order, and that, besides being gifted and children, they are lots of other things, too. We'd like them to experience other people, adults and children, whom they feel are worth listening to, folks who command enough natural respect from our kids because the kids know that they possess something worth learning. Folks with interesting hobbies, or occupations, or skills, or just unusual ways of seeing the world. We'd like our kids to meet up with other people who understand fun, and are willing to share it! And who appreciate that fun can mean different things for different people. And we want them to have the company of people who honor and respect their uniqueness, and that of everyone else, whether gifted or not. And, with them, and with us, we want our kids to have the opportunity to go out and explore the universe!

The truth is that our children are not going to be children forever, and that, except in very rarified circles, no one applies the term "gifted" to adults. At least they don't where I live. "Genius" perhaps, but almost always referring to a set of accomplishments, not to particular mental proclivities. "Gifted children" fade away and, with any luck, and lots of nurturing and kindness and respect, become ardent birdwatchers and knowledgeable gardeners, mathematical wizards, dependable postmen, creative architects. Formidable ballet dancers, moving folksingers, good cooks. Caring nurses, crafty detectives, talented inventors, trusted auto mechanics. Stamp collectors and weavers, poets and knitters. Loving fathers. Tenacious mothers. People who continue their knowledge quests on through their entire lives, and help open up the possibility of such quests for others with less in the way of opportunity. We all join the varied and universal pageant, and if we have been fortunate, we find a place in it that we can truly and comfortably call "home".

(And the older I get, the more I become convinced that "schooling" has very little to do with it.)

* * * * *

The best available resource for homeschooling with gifted kids is Lisa Rivero's *Creative Home Schooling: A Resource Guide for Smart Families* (Scottsdale, AZ: Great Potential Press, 2002). It is an exhaustive guide to the sights, sounds, and experiences that will enrich your journey together and it is also a good read. Even if you do not believe your child is intellectually gifted, this book will serve as a terrific resource for virtually any homeschooling family.

For those of you who wanted to explore giftedness issues still further, there are three websites I'd recommend:

- www.hoagiesgifted.org has a monthly newsletter, recommended articles and books, and lots of useful links.

- www.hollingworth.org is the website of the Hollingworth Center for Highly Gifted Children, one of the leading resource centers for gifted education in the U.S.

- www.tagfam.org is an extensive on-line community for families of talent and gifted children, with several on-line discussion groups. The TAGMAX list is for parents who homeschool gifted kids and fellow travelers.

She's Leaving Home

Sigh. My older daughter Aliyah, now 16, just left yesterday on her journey 3,000 miles away to college. I miss her already.

She's at Smith College, in Northampton, Massachusetts. She received their largest academic scholarship. Good thing, too, because we weren't going to be able to afford Smith on what my publishers pay me (hi, there! no, I'm *not* complaining, nor even angling for a raise), nor on what I take home from my day job. My wife is going back to school fulltime this fall to become a nurse. I won't be taking up a special collection any time soon (I do hope you buy my other books, though), and we've equipped Aliyah with a *real* winter coat (my mother kept offering her the raccoon—coat that is—if it were a live raccoon, Aliyah probably would have accepted, but the college says "No Pets Allowed.") Snowboots too. She won't be living on the street—in fact, the housing at Smith is downright gorgeous, and I wish my house looked like that!

The omens were unequivocal, I thought, when late last March I watched her begin to weave a thick wool, multicolored cloak, the kind that had New England written all over it. The scholarship letter arrived in the mail that afternoon.

"Funny," she said, pushing the shuttle through, "I lit a candle before the picture of Saraswati—the Indian goddess of wisdom—before I started to weave."

"Oh," I gulped, shivering at the notion that she lit candles in her firetrap of a room (what kids will do these days!) I then remembered that Sophia, the first name of Smith's founder, is the Greek goddess of wisdom, the western counterpart to Saraswati. I guess it was in the wind. Candles, votives, and incense are prohibited in the dorms at Smith College.

After she received the scholarship letter, I determined that I no longer had any right to demand that she clean her room. Not that I was ever particularly effective—I could get her to clean her room, which is far cry from saying that she ever actually got her room clean. Her college admissions essay (apparently effective) began, "My bedroom is an archeological dig," and went on to describe the flotsam and jetsam lying about, and then noted, "My mind is like my room." "Relics from my mind," she wrote, "like relics from the 'dig,' tend to turn up at strange and unpredictable intervals." She concluded:

In combing through the layers of my mind, I learn much about myself. My memories and the timing of their appearance are like pieces in a huge puzzle, that, when completed, will reveal me to myself, or so I hope. Perhaps there really is some organization in this messy aggregation, one that I cannot yet see from the inside but which has been there from the beginning, into which all these relics in my mind now fit, all in their proper places. The life of an archeologist of the mind is never dull.

So perhaps the room was supposed to be preserved, as is, as some kind of protected national treasure, open a few months each year to visiting scholars who possess special combing tools. I've secured a permit that allows me to take pictures. The loom is being shipped east as soon as Aliyah can figure out a place to park it.

We visited Smith together last April. Came prepared for snow squalls. The temperature never fell below 70 degrees in the daytime, and one day hit 88. So much for planning. I knew this was going to be interesting when the tour guide asked what her extracurriculars were, and Aliyah gave her a blank stare. It's not a word, or a distinction, we've ever made at home. But it was very clear upon first arrival that this was the place—when we drove into town, the only parking spot we could find turned up in front of the Northampton wool store!

Now what is she going to *do* there? Well, based on our visit, and her well-thumbed catalogue, she is like a kid in a candy store—with a no-limit credit card. (I'm not supposed to make any Smith Brothers cough drop jokes.) Notice I said, "do," as opposed to "study." Oh, yes, there is learning French, or will it be Italian? Read Dante in the original? Spend a year in Europe (which will it be, Florence or Paris? We are jealous, and want to come, too!) Write a symphony? (She's already got an opera under her belt, and wangled a job for herself as research assistant to the Five-College Opera Consortium.) Continue her forays into ethnobotany? Sing with the local opera company? Take organic chemistry and become a naturopath (on the side?) Get to the roots of Athenian democracy, or study the abolitionist history behind the Northampton silk mills? Plant an herb garden? Watch lots of foreign films? Learn how to snowshoe? Venture into astrophysics? Clerk a committee at the local Friends Meeting? Hike the Appalachian Trail? Lead a protest? Read Yiddish literature? Become an expert in Etruscan pottery? Knit lots of scarves?

Maybe all of the above? Sounds about eight years' worth. And maybe some things that neither she nor I can even imagine. Smith will just become part of the tapestry of her life, and, though at greater distance, ours. Couldn't ask for much better—Smith is an extraordinary place, so we don't mind *lending* Aliyah to them for awhile (as long as we still have visitation privileges.) But college will be just one more of those innumerable doors leading to the houses of sophia and, ultimately, as we all know when we allow ourselves the luxury to think about it, the most important doors swing inward.

Tomorrow my wife and I will wake up in the morning, and Aliyah won't be there. One less cup of coffee to make. Fewer travel plans to coordinate (though I'm working on a trip to India for Aliyah and me this January, where she will study traditional Tamil botanical medicine.) One less person to blame for the unwashed dishes in the sink, or the clothes strewn around the floor in the laundry room.

I thought long and hard about the send-off message. Sadly, I don't weave, or I would have made a wall hanging of it. Aliyah and my wife together spent several months sewing a going-away quilt. For me, it was a set of coffee mugs for some of her long nights ahead. And mine. I finally realized the message wasn't to be any different from that which has animated the rest of our homeschooling voyage, and our lives as well. Once I figured that out, the rest was easy:

> Have Fun.
> Learn Stuff.
> Grow.

Noah's Boat and the Pigeon of Peace

In the Jewish tradition in which I grew up, we have *midrashim*. A *midrash* is a parable or narrative interpretation or an interrogative dialogue with which one explores a sacred text, usually the stories to be found in the *Torah*—the Five Books of Moses—or the rest of the Old Testament.

A *midrash*, it should be understood, however, is not literary criticism. It is not an act of deconstruction, of rationally taking the words apart, or reducing it to some irreducible minimum. It is more an act of imagining oneself inside a sacred text, of imaginatively taking it into oneself even as one finds oneself enwrapped within it. Like a very noisy meditation, it is a way of encountering oneself in a new, previously unexplored context, while at the same time having the text take on the force of the present, even as it is rooted in the past. The text grows larger as a result, even as, if you've done it right, do you.

Sometimes I think that when I am contemplating our homeschooling adventures, I am writing *midrashim*. My children are the sacred texts, or at least the vessels for them. I encounter myself within them, even as I try to ensure their essence remains inviolate. Like most parents, I project my own hopes and dreams, successes and disappointments, expectations and excitement onto them. Sometimes I bring with me a healthy dose of perspective, and sometimes, well, I always urge parents to put some money into the therapy fund alongside the college one.

And then I remember that, as a living vessel of sacred texts as yet to be unfolded, each and every child is holy. Holy, not as something not to be touched, even if containing within them the spark of the transcendent, but as an ark, encompassing the wellsprings of future memories, those which will, someday, be inaccessible to me, but open to my grandchildren, or even those who come thereafter. Or perhaps, we are, together, a part of one unending scroll. As you can see, even in contemplating the art of *midrash*, I discover that I have written one.

And sometimes, more in keeping with the tradition, I find myself writing *midrashim* of the more traditional variety. Or, I am tempted to say, they write me. It is something I get to share with my children, who would be much less willing to put up with the more overtly philosophical ones. Maybe the literary equivalent of a hug. Here is my most recent, which poured out one Sunday, disrupting all of my plans for the rest of day, until it was sure I got it right.

* * * * *

(Based on a story by Isaac Baashevis Singer, itself based on a Yiddish folk tale, but told, shall we say, a little differently)

So God looked down upon the earth, and saw that it hadn't actually turned out the way He had planned. "I must be able to do better than this," He thought, rubbing His eyes after having peered through His binoculars for too long.

But He remembered how hard He'd labored over the animals. What, had it taken Him *a whole day*? And He was kind of happy with them. Some were even cute and cuddly. And so He decided that while He'd destroy everything else, He'd keep the furry and feathered and etceteras, the fish could fend for themselves, and He'd give it another try. Level everything, erase it like a blackboard, and start over.

He decided He'd entrust the animals to Noah, who seemed to be mostly unemployed for the past century, and so had plenty of time on his hands.

"Noah," He said.

"Whoah," replied Noah, awakening from his half-slumber and stroking his long, scraggly beard, "What's that?"

"Noah," God spoke with authority, "Build ye an ark."

Now Noah was already four hundred and something years old, but he hadn't heard anybody say "ye" in an very, very long time, so he figured it must be God talking because no one else he knew spoke that way.

"Yes, Lord?" Noah said, sitting up, and feeling a little tipsy from his hangover from the night before.

"I said," repeated God, now just a little annoyed, "Build ye an ark."

"What's an ark?" asked Noah sheepishly, opening up his arms and raising his hands palms out.

"It's a kind of boat," spake the Lord.

"Boat? Why would anyone need a boat around here? There's not much water or anything. Just a piddling little stream. You mean like a canoe?"

"No, a big boat," said the Lord, "Big enough to put all the animals in."

"Won't it smell?" asked Noah, expressing uncertainty about the whole venture.

"You're going to have bigger problems than that to think about," replied God, getting a little steamy, and handing him the blueprints. "Now get to work."

So Noah pondered the plans. He'd never built anything before in his life, or at least nothing particularly substantial. The blueprints called for cubits of this and that, and Noah had no idea what a cubit was, but he decided to make believe he'd figure it out once he got started.

It was pretty slow-going at first. The local lumberyard and hardware store never seemed to have what he needed, and everything had to be special ordered. It cost him a pretty penny.

But slowly it began to take shape, though what shape it was supposed to be Noah had no idea. When he told his curious friends that it was an ark, there was great skepticism (no one ever having heard of an ark before, and there wasn't any body of water within two hundred miles). They were all convinced it wouldn't float.

At last, the ark was completed, and the animals all gathered to come aboard. But it sure looked awfully small.

"You'll have to take me," said the giraffe, assuming Noah was going to have to pick and choose. "Just knock a little hole in the ceiling and I can be the lookout."

"Well, you'll want me—I'm the largest, and have the longest trunk," said the elephant.

"I'm the fattest," said the hippopotamus, also indicating that the world would suffer a great loss without something named "hippopotamus" in it. "Besides, I have the biggest mouth."

"Not likely," said the alligator yawning, its jaws open three cubits wide.

"I'm the king of the jungle," opined the lion, assuring himself that no place could exist for very long without a king.

"I have the best wool," said the lamb, and then perceiving potential problems, "Just put me on the other side of the boat from the lion."

"I am closest to the earth," said the snake, not being able to figure out anything else in particular to recommend himself.

"You forgot me!" cried the earthworm.

"How many other birds can quack?" said the duck.

"I can talk like a human, and keep you company," said the parrot.

"I am the most beautiful, and have the most beautiful eyes," said the horse, batting her beautiful eyelids at Noah.

"But you only have two of them; look at these babies!" said the horsefly, with literally thousands of eyes on each side of his head.

Off to the side, Noah saw a little gray bird sitting quietly, just minding his own business.

"What about you, dove? asked Noah.

"Oh, please, none of this dove business, thank you, nothing so fancy-shmancy. I'm just a pigeon," he replied quietly, adjusting the bill of his cap. "Nothing special about me. Just a regular guy. I do what I need to get by. But if you give me a little space up in the rafters in the back, don't worry, I won't make any trouble."

And then Noah remembered that God hadn't said anything about selecting which animals to take, and came to the conclusion that he was supposed to take them all.

"Even the mosquitoes?" whinnied the horse, expressing a view shared by many of the others.

"Mosquitoes, too," replied Noah.

And so on they went, with a little judicious planning and a lot of pushing and shoving, they all got on. It wasn't pretty, but this was no cruise ship.

And the rains came. Forty days and forty nights it rained. It didn't rain cats and dogs—they were already on the boat, which, surprising even to Noah, didn't leak at all. And the earth was erased like a blackboard, and then the rain stopped. The sun came out. The boat came to rest on top of a big... well, they weren't quite sure what it was yet. The giraffe craned his neck out the top like a periscope, but all he could see was water everywhere.

"Someone's going to have to go out and take a look around," said Noah.

"Not I," said the giraffe, "If my legs don't feel the ground, I just flail around. Watching a giraffe try to swim is not a pretty sight."

"Not I," said the snake, "Water gives me the creeps!"

"Limited range," said the duck, "I can paddle around this here, what did you call it, ah, yes, ark, but that's about all you can expect out of me."

"I'm solely a jungle person," yawned the lion, still eyeing the lamb on the other side of the boat.

And so it went. Each of them had their reasons.

And then Noah turned to the d...pigeon.

"Well, someone's gotta go," sighed the pigeon from up in the rafters, pulling his cap tight on his head. "So it might as well be me."

And out he went. A couple of days later he came back, bareheaded. His wings were a bit wet, and in the sun, they shone iridescent, like a rainbow. He was still a pigeon, but he'd come back...changed. And in his mouth he carried an olive branch.

"Peace," he said. "Peace. Flying around out there, I got this message. It's a big earth. Bigger, and greener, and more beautiful than ever before. Plenty of room for all of us, if we can just figure out how to live together. Hey, if we can manage for forty days and forty nights on this here smelly ark, the rest should be a piece of cake, don't you think? And he flew off.

And Noah and the animals made their way off as well, each going his own way. All trying to remember that it really is possible to get along.

And on that day, God made a decision. From that day forth, when He had a message to send, He wasn't going to entrust it to the biggest, or the strongest, or the kingliest, or the best talker, or the one with the biggest mouth. He was going to make sure to entrust His message to just a regular guy. Nobody special. No doves—nothing fancy-shmancy—just pigeons. Just like me and you.

And He was going to make sure there were plenty of pigeons in the cities, so that we could remember the rainbow sign.

And peace to you!

Appendix

"On Schools"

John Woolman

First published in 1758 by Philadelphia Yearly Meeting, Religious Society of Friends, as part of a series titled "Considerations on Pure Wisdom, and Human Policy; on Labor; on Schools; and on the Right Use of the Lord's Outward Gifts"

* * * * *

Suffer the little children to come unto me, and forbid them not, for of such is the kingdom of God."

– Mark X. 14

To encourage children to do things with a view to get praise of men appears an obstruction to their being inwardly acquainted with the spirit of truth. For it is the work of the Holy Spirit to direct the mind to God; that in all our proceeding we may have a single eye to Him; may give alms in secret; fast in secret; and labor to keep clear of that disposition reproved by our Savior, "But all their works they do for to be seen of men." – Matthew XXIII. 5.

That Divine light which enlightens all men, does, I believe, often shine in the minds of children very early; and humbly to wait for wisdom that our conduct towards them may tend to forward their acquaintance with it, and strengthen them in obedience thereto, appears to me to be a duty on us all. By cherishing in them the spirit of pride, and the love of praise, I believe they may sometimes improve faster in learn than they otherwise would; but to take measures to forward children in learning, which naturally tend to divert their minds from true humility, appears to me to savor of the wisdom of this world. If tutors are not acquainted with sanctification of spirit, nor experienced in an humble waiting for the leadings of truth, but follow the maxims of the wisdom of this world, such children as are under their tuition, appear to me to be in danger of imbibing thoughts and habits the reverse of that meekness and lowliness of heart, which is necessary for all the true followers of Christ.

Children at an age fit for schools, are at a time of life which requires the patient attention of pious people; and if we commit them to the tuition of those, whose minds we believe are not rightly prepared to "train them up in the nurture and admonition of the Lord," we are in danger of not acting the part of faithful parents toward them. Our heavenly Father doth not require us to do evil that good may come of it; and it is needful that we deeply examine ourselves, lest we get entangled in the wisdom of this world, and through wrong apprehensions, take such methods of our children. It is a lovely sight to behold innocent children; and when they are sent to schools where their tender minds are in imminent danger of being led astray by tutors, who do not live a self-denying life, or by the conversation of such children as do not live in innocence, it is a case much to be lamented.

While a pious tutor hath the charge of no more children than he can take due care of, and keeps his authority in the truth, the good spirit in which he leads and governs, works on the minds of such as are not hardened; and his labors not only tend to bring them forward and outward learning, but to open their understandings with respect of the true Christian life; but when a person hath charge of too many, and his thoughts and time are so much employed in the outward affairs of his school, that he does not so weightily attend to the spirits and conduct of each individual, as to be enabled to administer rightly to all in due season; through such omission, he not only suffers as to the state of his own mind, but the minds of his children are in danger of suffering also.

To watch the spirits of children, to nurture them in gospel love, and labor to help them against that which would mar the beauty of their minds, is a debt we owe them; and a faithful performance of our duty not only tends to their lasting benefit, and to our own peace, but also renders their company agreeable to us. Instruction thus administered, reaches the pure witness in the minds of such children as are not hardened, and begets love in them towards those who thus lead them on; but where too great a number are committed to one tutor, and he, through much cumber, omits a careful attention to the minds of his scholars, there is danger of disorders gradually increasing among them, until they grow too strong to be easily remedied. A care hath lived on my mind, that more time might be employed by parents at home, and by tutors at school, in weightily attending to the spirit and inclinations of children, and that we may so lead, instruct, and govern them, in this tender part of life, that nothing may be omitted which it is in our power, to help them on their way to becoming the children of our Father who is in heaven.

Meditating on the situation of schools in our provinces, my mind hath at times been affected with sorrow; and under this exercise, it hath appeared to me, that if those who have large estates were faithful stewards, and laid no rent, nor interest, nor other demand, higher than is consistent with universal love; and if those in lower circumstances would under a moderate employ, shun unnecessary expense, even to the smallest article; and all unite humbly seeking to the Lord, He would graciously instruct, and strengthen us to relieve the youth from various snares in which many of them are entangled.

About the Author

David H. Albert is a homeschooling dad, writer, storyteller, and author of *Homeschooling and the Voyage of Self-Discovery* (Common Courage Press, 2003); A*nd the Skylark Sings with Me: Adventures in Homeschooling and Community Based-Education* (New Society Publishers, 1999); editor of a new book about his Indian parents *The Color of Freedom* (Common Courage Press, 2005); as well as two books about the uses of storytelling, *The Healing Heart~Families* and *The Healing Heart~Communities* (New Society Publishers, 2003). He writes a regular column—"My Word! —for Home Education Magazine, and a

David as "the inspired author" in Opera Pacifica's production of *I Pagliacci* by Ruggiero Leoncavallo, April 2005. Photo by Ellen Sawislak.

second column—"What Really Matters"—with Joyce Reed, for The Link. His work has appeared in scores of magazines and journals worldwide, ranging from Life Learning Magazine to the Journal of the American Philosophical Society. As founder of New Society Publishers, he was both editor and publisher of John Taylor Gatto's *Dumbing Us Down: The Hidden Curriculum of Compulsory Schooling*, and more than a 100 other titles. He was also a founding member of Co-op America and the National Association of Socially Responsible Businesses.

David lives in Olympia, Washington with his wife and partner Ellen and younger daughter Meera (age 15). His older daughter Aliyah (18) is an undergraduate at Smith College in Northampton, Massachusetts, majoring in music composition. He holds degrees from Williams College, Oxford University, and the University of Chicago, but says the best education he ever received he gets from his kids. When he is not learning with and from children, writing, making music, or raising funds for community development projects in south India, he serves as Senior Planning and Policy Analyst for the Washington State Division of Alcohol and Substance Abuse. David is also an active member of the Religious Society of Friends (Quakers), and moderator of the Quaker Homeschooling Circle.

David is available for speaking engagements or workshops in your community. He invites your comments as well. Write him at shantinik@earthlink.net or visit his website at www.skylarksings.com

About the Cover Artist

Brianna K. Thomas created the cover out of Plasticine when she was 15. She is homeschooled and loves to draw, write, paint and sing—anything creative. She is also a yellow belt in Judo. She lives with her family in British Columbia, Canada.